THE
TRAVELS AND ADVENTURES

THE TRAVELS AND ADVENTURES

OF THE TURKISH ADMIRAL

SIDI ALI REÏS

IN INDIA, AFGHANISTAN, CENTRAL ASIA, AND PERSIA, DURING THE YEARS 1553-1556

TRANSLATED FROM THE TURKISH, WITH NOTES

A. VAMBERY

Published by

GYAN

Gyan Publishing House
5, Ansari Road
Daryaganj, New Delhi-110002
Phone: 011-47034999, 9811692060
E-mail: books@gyanbooks.com

Distribution Network
gyanbooks.com
India, USA, Canada, UK, Australia

ISBN: 978-93-7414-377-3 (PB)

First Published, 1899

2nd Impression 2026

Printed at: Gyan Press, Delhi.

THE TRAVELS AND ADVENTURES
Translated by: A.VAMBERY

THE
TRAVELS AND ADVENTURES
OF THE TURKISH ADMIRAL
SIDI ALI REÏS

IN INDIA, AFGHANISTAN, CENTRAL ASIA, AND PERSIA, during the Years 1553—1556.

THE TRAVELS AND ADVENTURES OF THE TURKISH ADMIRAL SIDI ALI REÏS

IN INDIA, AFGHANISTAN, CENTRAL ASIA, AND PERSIA,
during the Years 1553—1556.

TRANSLATED FROM THE TURKISH, WITH NOTES,

BY

A. VAMBÉRY.

LONDON:
LUZAC & Co.
Publishers to the India Office.
1899.

CONTENTS.

Chap. Page.

Introduction . . . . I.

Preface of the Turkish Publisher . . . . XI.

I. . . . . 1.

II. The Beginning of the Story . . . . 2.

III. About what happened in Basrah . . . . . . 7.

IV. What took place in the Sea of Ormuz. . . . . 9.

V. What we suffered in the Indian Ocean . . . . . . 17.

VI. What happened in the Province of Gujarat . . . . 24.

VII. What befell us in the Province of Sind . . . . . 36.

VIII. My Experiences in Hindustan. . . . . 45.

[1] XI. Our Experience in Bakhtar-Zemin, i. e. in Kabulistan. 63.

XII. The Condition of Badakshan and Khatlan. . . . . 66.

XIII. Events in Turan, i. e. Transoxania . . . . 68.

XIV. Our Experiences in Kharezm and Deshti-Kipchak . . 79.

XV. Our Fate in Khorasan . . . . 84.

XVI. Our Vicissitudes in Irak-Adjem . . . . 90.

XVII. The rest of our Adventures. . . . . 103.

---

1 The Chapters have been erroneously numbered; there are only fifteen chapters in all.

INTRODUCTION.

The little book of the Turkish Admiral Sidi Ali Reïs [1], entitled "Mirat ūl Memalik" (the Mirror of

[1] This work has long since been known in the East, and a German Translation of it by Heinrich Friedrich von Diez appeared in his „Memoirs of Asia" (Denkwürdigkeiten von Asien) II, pp. 733—267, which translation was afterwards rendered into French by Morris, and published in the Journal Asiatique IX, 27—299 and X, 46—112. The reasons that in spite of all this I have ventured to make a fresh translation, are briefly the following: 1. The Berlin Orientalist, Ambassador Extraordinary and Minister Plenipotentiary, had only a written copy of the "Weltenspiegel" (Mirror of the World) at his disposal, while I have had access to the latest printed Edition [a]) published in Constantinople, and consequently was not so likely to be led astray by the uncertainties and variations in the Oriental manuscript. 2. Our knowledge of the Turkish Language has considerably increased since Diez's publication in 1815 and many of the discrepancies and inaccuracies of his translation could now be avoided. 3. The Geography and History of the countries concerned have now

---

a) The exact title of the work as it appeared in Stambul in 1895 is as follows:

Ikdam Library. A work of ancient authors, viz. The Mirror of Countries, written by Sidi Ali Reïs and edited by Ahmed Djevdet, editor and proprietor of the Ikdam newspaper. Printed by permission of the Ministry of Public Instruction in the Printing Office of the Ikdam in Stambul 1313 (1895). Price two piasters.

Countries), is in many ways very interesting. In the first place on account of the personality of the author, in whom we see a man of many varied accomplishments; a genuine type of the Islamitic culture of his time and a representative of that class of official and military dignataries to whose influence it is chiefly due that the Ottoman empire, extending over three continents, attained to that eminent height of culture which it occupied during the reign of Suleiman the Great. Sidi Ali is the descendant of an illustruous family connected with the arsenal at Galata, in whom love for the sea seems to have been hereditary, and hence, as the Turkish publisher points out in his preface, Sidi Ali, being thoroughly acquainted with the nautical science of his day, excels as author on maritime subjects.

As a man of general culture, he was in harmony with the prevailing notions of his time, as mathematician, astronomer and geographer; and also as poet, theologian and in all branches of general literature;

assumed quite a different aspect, the original text of the travelling account of the Turkish Admiral, can therefore be understood and explained much more clearly. Besides all this the extensive English Literature of the present day on Indian Topics and my personal experiences when travelling in those countries, have been of great help to me; I have therefore thought it incumbent upon me to prepare a fresh translation, but for obvious reasons I have refrained from any critical comments on Diez's rendering.

sometimes wielding his pen in writing lyrical or occasional verses, at other times entering into keen controversial disputes upon certain Koran-theses or burning schismatic questions.

Besides all this he was a warrior, proving himself as undaunted in fighting the elements as in close combat with the Portuguese, who in point of accoutrement had far the advantage over him. But what stands out above all these accomplishments, is his glowing patriotism and his unwavering faith in the power and the greatness of the Ottoman empire. He boasts that he never ceases to hope to see Gujarat and Ormuz joined to the Ottoman realm; his one desire is to see his Padishah ruler of the world, and wherever he goes and whatever he sees, Rum (Turkey) always remains in his eyes, the most beautiful, the richest, and the most cultured land of the whole world. The Turkish Admiral has moreover a singularly happy way of expressing himself on this subject of his preference for his own Padishah and his native land; and this required no small amount of courage and tact where he had to face proud Humayun or Thamasp no less conceited than the former.

With regard to the things which he saw and heard in non-musulman circles and districts in India, his accounts are poor compared with the descriptions of Ibn Batūtā and other moslem travellers. Sidi Ali has had hardly any intercourse with Hindus, and his route lay almost entirely through districts, where the ruling caste, with whom he principally had to deal, were adherents to the mohammedan faith. It does appear somewhat strange that he had such unbounded reverence for the Sultan of Turkey, and upheld him as the legitimate caliph, although the caliphate had only fallen into the hands of the Ottoman rulers, a few years previously with the overthrow of Tuman Bey by Selim II; and this seems the more strange, as Asia is so tenaciously conservative that even to this day the Turkish claim to the caliphate is a disputed point.

The authoritative and executive power of Turkey, formerly the terror of the Christian world, could not fail to exercise its influence upon the Moslem lands of Asia and their unstable governments, torn and harrassed as they were by internal strife and petty wars, while the sultans of Turkey basked, not only in the glory of spiritual preferment, but also in that of temporal superiority. The picture which our author draws of the government of India and the East is certainly a very sad one. Civil wars and mutinies against the rulers of the land are every day occurrences; the roads swarm with highwaymen, and even during the reign of the much-extolled Humayun, all intercourse with other lands was fraught with every imaginable kind of danger. Their rulers all suffer from a peculiar form of conceit, like the ruler of Bokhara, who asked me, pointing to a ragged motley crowd of ruffians, whether the army of the Sultan of Turkey were not exactly like this. Humayun, Thamasp, and even Borak Khan of Bokhara, all delighted in drawing parallels between themselves and Sultan Suleiman.

One thing however in the account of the Turkish Admiral is certainly surprising, namely the few facts by which he illustrates the Sultan's policy in Moslem Asia. We have always been under the impression that the Turks, during the era of their supreme power and universal sway, directed their attention more towards the Christian lands of the West, than towards the Moslem lands of the East, and that as a matter of fact their campaigns were nothing short of marauding raids, and empty conquests, while they might have utalised the many means at their disposal and the high prestige in which they stood towards the consolidation of their power in Asia, which would have been comparatively easy. This reproach is neither unfounded nor unmerited, for although the finest of the Ottoman rulers, Sultan Selim, did direct his attention chiefly towards the East, as proved by his campaigns against Persia and Egypt, most of his predecessors and successors have occupied themselves solely in making war in the West. Asia, which offered little to tempt the mercinary janissaries, was meanwhile left pretty well to its own devices, without any fixed form or plan of government. — But, as in this narrative the threads of the policy pursued by those sultans, one by one come to light, we are struck with the fact that after all they were not quite so short-sighted as we gave them credit for, and that now and again they have given a thought to the bringing about of a better state of things.

In one of my earlier works [1] I pointed out that Sultan Ahmed II, who had not been very successful in war, had entered into negotiations with the rulers of Transoxania, and, together with them, had vowed the destruction of the Shiite world, which had wedged itself into the body of the Sunnite community. Sultan Suleiman went much further; he aimed at the subjugation of the whole of the then existing Moslem East, hence his diplomacy in the Arabian and Persian seas, and his deep-laid plans for taking Ormuz from the Portuguese in order to obtain a firm footing in Gujarat. If this plan had succeeded, he would have broken the growing power of the successors of Baber and established himself as sole ruler of Hindustan. If Suleiman, instead of deluging Hungary and Austria with his janissaries, had put

[1] Vambéry, Geschichte Bokhara II, 130.

the conquest of India on his programme, his efforts would have been crowned with greater and more lasting success than that which attended them in the Danubian provinces. He had at his disposal a mighty, ever victorious fleet, while the descendants of Baber were entirely without one. His prestige was great and without parallel in Arabia, Egypt, nay even in the whole of the Islam world, and the victory which a handful of Central Asian adventurers could obtain over the Vishnū worshippers, would have been child's play to his disciplined, well-armed, valiant bands of Janissaries. The Ottoman rulers as masters of India would have played a far more important part in history than any of their predecessors on the road to conquest, and who can say what might not have been the fate of Asia under such conditions?

Simultaneously with India, Suleiman had also directed his attention towards the countries of the Oxus, as proved by the sending of 300 Janissaries to Bokhara to organize the military forces of Borak Khan, in order to secure for him superiority over his rivals. Most characteristic are the ways and means employed to smuggle these Ottoman soldiers, from the shores of the Bosphorus to the distant banks of the Zarafshan. To allay the suspicions of the Persian Monarch it was said that the Turks had merely served as an escort to the pious Sheikh Abdullatif, on his long journey over the Caucasus, the Caspian sea and across the steppes of the Khirgiz. But this was not the case, for as we learn from the narrative of Sidi Ali, they had entered the service of Borak Khan, took part in his battles and did not leave him until they had realized the futility of their efforts. Borak Khan himself had been unpleasantly undeceived, and his expression that he was ashamed of his inability to keep his word to the Sultan, suggests at any rate, some secret understanding between the Porte and himself.

Between the shores of the Black Sea and the boundaries of China there was still plenty of scope for work for the Ottoman realm, which had just secured a foothold on the threshold of Europe. The people of the Caucasus (the western Caucasus) were not yet won over to Islam, for it was not until the XVIIth century that Ferrukh Pasha was sent out to convert the Circassians to Islam. The Kirghizes also were as yet Infidels, for why otherwise should our travellers be told at Bokhara that the Kirghizes treated the musulmans badly. Moslem writers certainly do speak of the conversion of the Caucasus and Central Asia, as early as the first century of Hijra; but this should be understood to refer only to the cities and settled inhabitants, and even to them with reservations; the nomadic and military contingents of those countries, however, were not converted to Islam, until much later, and on certain points they are even to this day, Mohammedans only in name.

For the rest, even in modern times, there has been no lack of evidence of the curious dealings of the Porte with the Sunnites in the Far East. About the middle of the forties, Sultan Abdul Medjid sent the Khan of Bokhara some soldiers drilled according to the modern school, to assist him in establishing a regular army there. The same thing was done to assist the Atalik Ghazi, i. e. Yakub Kushbeghi, the ruler of Eastern Turkestan, who expelled the Chinese from his territory and founded a kingdom at Kashgar. In both cases however the attempt failed. The spirit of strong conservatism was too deeply rooted in the Asiatic mind, to allow their old-world notions to be superceded by modern ideas of warfare, and the musulmans, sent on that mission, returned unsuccessful.

The notes of Sidi Ali's travels, are full of traits of this sort, and from them it is quite easy to conjure up a picture of Moslem Asia in the XVIth century. As for his style and language, it seems that he expresses himself more easily in verse than in prose, for the latter is often almost unintelligible.

His language betrays the influence of his year's residence in Central Asia, for he makes use of words and expressions, which are not current in the Ottoman literature of his time, and are totally unknow to the western Turks.

In the following translation, my principal object has been, not so much to assist Orientalists in their researches, but rather Geographers and Ethnographers, and I have therefore omitted all superfluous, flowery speeches, synonyms, and bombast non-essential to the right understanding of the text. Neither have I attempted to translate the verses inserted in the original. These are written for the greater part in the Djagatai language and are of no general interest, repeating ad nauseum the imagery and methaphors of Oriental poetry, and containing absolutely nothing in any way relating to the course of events or to the places and peoples with which this narrative is concerned.

A. VAMBÉRY.

PREFACE OF THE TURKISH PUBLISHER.

When Sultan Suleiman resided in Bagdad in the year 945 (1538) there appeared at his court a certain Mani, son of Makas Ogli Mir Rashid, the ruler of Basrah; he came with rich gifts to present the keys of that town, and the Sultan was pleased to honour him with a grand reception. In the year 837 (1433)[1] Khadim Suleiman Pasha, Beglerbeg of Egypt, distinguished for his naval and military accomplishments, had fitted out at Suez, a fleet for the conquest of Yemen and Aden, when he was summoned to join the Imperial army then starting on its campaign to Bagdad. In acknowledgment of his services there the dignity of Vizier had been bestowed upon him, and upon the completion of the campaign, he was reinstated in his former position. It was about this time that Humayun Shah, a descendant of Sultan Baber, who had made vast conquests in India and

[1] More correctly 937 (1530).

incorporated many districts into his realm, marched against Bahadur Shah, the ruler of Gujarat, who immediately sent an envoy with suitable gifts to Sultan Suleiman, soliciting his Imperial protection. At the time that this envoy appeared at the court in Adrianople, i. e. in the year 943 (1536), the Portuguese availed themselves of the war between Humayun and Bahadur Shah, to take possession of Bender-i-Diw, situated within the dominion of Gujarat. When Suleiman Pasha heard this, he left Suez on the 15th of Moharram of the Year 945 (1538) with a well-equipped fleet of 80 vessels. Impressed by the sight of this mighty fleet the ruler of Aden, Amir bin Daūd, had volontarily yielded to the protection of the Padishah, and so this stronghold was incorporated into the Ottoman empire without striking a blow. From there the fleet sailed on to Gujarat and after a successful battle, the two strongholds Kükele and Ket[1] were taken from the Portuguese. The fleet then proceeded to Bender-i-Diw. Bahadur Shah meanwhile had died and was succeeded by Melik Mahmud. When he was told that the fleet had arrived for his protection and that he was expected to provide it with food and ammunition, Melik Mahmud, deluded by the promises of the

[1] On English maps given as Keti-bender, (Harbour of Ket), in the district of Karachi.

Portuguese, refused to render them any assistance, and so, although the outworks of the strong fortress which on three sides was surrounded by the sea, were already in possession of the valiant musulman sailors, the undertaking had to be given up and the fleet was compelled to retire.

After the conquest of Egypt, the provinces of Yemen and Arabistan, formerly subject to the Circassians (Mameluks), came under Turkish rule, and, without the help of any Ottoman force, the government of those provinces was entrusted to a Circassian, called Iskender Bey and a Turk called Ramazan Bey. There the matter was left. After the change of government the Circassians immediately donned the Turkish garb and together with the Rumi (West Turks) adopted the epithet 'Mahzarin' [1] and used their power as they pleased. They even ventured to oppose Suleiman Pasha, the commander of the fleet, who thereupon took captive the Nakhuda [2], called Ahmed, and placed in his stead Mustafa Bey, the son of Biyikli Mehemmed Pasha, formerly governor of Diarbekir, and thus succeeded in restoring order.

[1] Mahzarin, means literally, yellow, faded or withered and refers to the new shoots from the seed of a plant. Iskender Bey and the other Circassians (Mameluks) whose last ray of hope had been well nigh extinguished, but who were now restored to office, were designated by this epithet.

[2] Literally shipscaptain.

It was therefore, remembering the consequences of this earlier campaign and with a view to the complete annexation of Arabia, that Sultan Suleiman decided upon the present course, and formed the plan to take the island of Ormuz and revenge himself upon the Portuguese.

The execution of this plan was entrusted to Piri Bey the Egyptian Admiral, who accordingly, in the year 961 (1553) set out from Suez to Ormuz with 30 ships, galleys and bashtardas. He immediately prepared for the siege, but when he saw that the Portuguese had a far superior force at their disposal, he sent the fleet, entrusted to his care, to Basrah, and he himself returned to Suez with three vessels. This inactivity on the part of Piri Bey, was attributed to bribery in certain circles where he was not liked, and in consequence of this he was put to death. It was to replace him that the command of the fleet was entrusted to the Galataen, Sidi Ali Reis, the author of this little book, which forms the third volume of the "Mirror of Countries" series, published by the "Ikdam" Library.

There was a time, when amongst the commanders and officers of the Ottoman naval and military forces, men were to be found, who distinguished themselves with the pen as well as with the sword. Sidi Ali Reis was one of these and although the navy and its accompanying sciences was his special sphere of knowledge, he also excelled most of his contemporaries in poetry and composition. He was known under the fictitious name of "Kiatibi" or Kiatibi Rum [1]. In 960 (1552) he accompanied Sultan Suleiman Kanuni on his eastern campaign to Aleppo. In 961 (1553) he was appointed to the post of Admiral of the Egyptian fleet (Missr Kapudanligi), and commanded to fetch back from Basrah the fleet which Piri Bey had left there.

He proceeded thither by land, but when he prepared to leave Basrah with the fleet, the Portuguese, ever victorious in those waters, had attacked him. This misfortune, aggravated by a severe storm which ran several of his vessels to the ground, frustated all his plans, and he barely escaped with the few remaining vessels to the coast of Gujarat. Leaving his ships in charge of the ruler of the place, he travelled by land over Sind, Punjab, Afghanistan Transoxania, Khorassan, Azerbijan, and through Persia. Wherever he came the Mahommedan rulers presented to him addresses of loyalty and devotion to

[1] i. e. Turkish writer.

the Padishah, and at last he reached Constantinople, via Bagdad, in the year 964. These four years of compulsory travel have been recorded by Sidi Ali Reis in a book called „Mirat ŭl Memalik", (Mirror of Countries), and when he presented it to the Sultan, he was restored (?) to favour. At first he received a daily pay of 80 Akche's, and the title of "Mūte-ferrika" (Officer in attendance on the Sultan), and shortly after he was raised to the office of Timar-Defterdar of Diarbekir; he died in 980 (1572). Sidi Reis was the son of Husein Reis, Steward of the Imperial Arsenal then at Galata, whose father and grandfather had occupied the same post. Sidi Reis therefore, belonged to one of the most distinguished families of his time and as he had inherited an insatiable love for the sea, he had taken part in most of the naval engagements of the time under such famous navigators as Khaireddin (Barbarossa) and Sinan Pasha. He wrote five treatises upon the Astrolabe, the Quadrant ربع مجيب, the parallels مقنطرات, the manufacture and the use of.....[1] and under the title of "Mirat-ul Kainat" (the Mirror of Creation) he wrote an interesting pamphlet upon the theory and practice of Nautical science. During his residence in Ahmedabad he wrote a book called "Muhit", in

[1] In the text معدل وذات الكرسى Inu'adil we zat-el-Kursi (?)

which he gives much information upon the Gulf of Oman, and a German translation of which was given by Baron Hammer of Vienna. The Turkish original will also shortly be published.

The "Mirat ūl Memalik" (Mirror of Countries) has so far not been published in its entirety and the loose copies extent are far too few in number to be accessible to the knowledge-loving public. The fragment here presented has been fully discussed in the German Newspapers under the heading "Indisch asiatische Kenntnisse." The copy which I have used was the gift of Abdullah Bey, the great scholar, especially learned in ancient Manuscripts, to the Editor of the 'Ikdam' [1]. Sidi Reis who had learned Djagatai-Turkish in the course of his travels, has written several Ghazels and Chronogramms in this dialect. He presented these to different Turkish princes, principally to Humayun Shah, who called him a second Mir Ali Shir. Sidi Reis, therefore, ranks amongst the first Ottoman Oriental scholars. He was universally known for his gentleness and high-mindedness, and his house in Galata was famous for its hospitality and liberality.

[1] The first vol. of Tarikhi Perchĕvi (Pechevi ?) which was published by the express wish of the late Ghalib Bey a famous osman scholar and son of Edhem Pasha, contains an extract from the book now before us.

In conclusion I consider it my duty to offer my sincere thanks to the publishers and printers of the "Ikdam Library" for the publication of this work, with which they have conferred so large a benefit upon science.

NEDJIB AASIM.

I.

When Sultan Suleiman had taken up his winter-residence in Aleppo, I, the author of these pages, was appointed to the Admiralship of the Egyptian fleet, and received instructions to fetch back to Egypt, the ships (15 galleys), which some time ago had been sent to Basrah on the Persian Gulf. But, 'Man proposes, God disposes.' I was unable to carry out my mission, and as I realized the impossibility of returning by water, I resolved to go back to Turkey by the overland route, accompanied by a few tried and faithful Egyptian soldiers. I travelled through Gujarat, Hind, Sind, Balkh, Zabulistan, Bedakhshan, Khotlan, Turan, and Iran, i. e. through Transoxania, Khorassan, Kharezm, and Deshti-Kiptchak; and as I could not proceed any further in that direction, I went by Meshed and the two Iraks, Kazwin and Hamadan, on to Bagdad.

Our travels ended, my companions and fellow-adventurers persuaded me to write down our experiences, and the dangers through which we had passed, an accurate account of which it is almost impossible to give; also to tell of the cities and the many wonderful sights we had seen, and of the holy shrines we had visited. And so this little book sees the light; in it I have tried to relate in simple and plain language, the troubles and difficulties, the suffering and the distress which beset our path, up to the time that we reached Constantinople. Considering the matter it contains this book ought to have been entitled, "A tale of woe," but with a view to the scene of action I have called it "Mirror of Countries," and as such I commend it to the reader's kind attention.

II.

The beginning of the story.

When the illustrious Padishah was holding his court at Aleppo, in Ramazan of the year 960 (1552), I was commanded to join the army.

I celebrated Ramzam-Bairam in attendance on His Majesty, later on however, I went to Sidi-Ghazi, made a pilgrimage in Konia to the tomb of Molla-i-Rŭmi, and visited the shrines of the Sultan ul-Ulema, and Shemsi Tebrizi, and of the Sheikh's Sadr-ed-din-

Koniavi; at Kassarie I made a pilgrimage to the graves of the Sheikh's Awhad-ed-din Kirmani, Burham-ed-din, Baha-ed-din Zade, Ibrahim Akserayi and Davud Kaissari. Returned to Haleb (Aleppo), I visited the graves of Daud, Zakeriah and Balkiah, as also those of Saad and Said, companions of the Prophet. The Kurban-Bairam I spent again in attendance on the Sultan.

I must here mention that Piri Bey, the late Admiral of the Egyptian fleet, had, some time previous to this, been dispatched with about 30 ships[1] (galleys and galleons) from Suez, through the Red sea, touching Jedda and Yemen, and through the straits of Bab-i-Mandeb, past Aden and along the coast of Shahar[2]. Through fogs and foul weather his fleet became dispersed, some ships were lost, and with the remainder he proceeded from Oman to Muscat, took the fortress and made all the inhabitants prisoners; he also made an incursion into the islands of Ormuz and Barkhat, after which he returned to Muscat. There he learned from the captive Infidel captain that the Christian (Portuguese) fleet was on its way, that therefore any further delay was inadvisable, as in case it arrived he would not be able to leave

[1] In the text these are specified as Bashtarda, Kadirga, Kalta and Kalium.

[2] Shahar is the name of the coastline between Oman and Aden.

the harbour at all. As a matter of fact it was already too late to save all the ships; he therefore took only three, and with these just managed to make his escape before the arrival of the Portuguese. One of his galleys was wrecked near Bahrein, so he brought only two vessels back to Egypt. As for the remainder of the fleet at Basrah, Kubad Pasha had offered the command of it to the Chief Officer, but he had declined, and returned to Egypt by land.

When this became known in Constantinople the command of the fleet had been given to Murad Bey formerly Sanjakbey of Catif, then residing in Basrah. He was ordered to leave two ships, five galleys, and one galleon at Basrah and with the rest, i. e. 15 galleys (one galley had been burned in Basrah) and two boats, he was to return to Egypt. Murad Bey did start as arranged, but opposite Ormuz he came upon the Infidel (Portuguese) fleet, a terrible battle followed in which Suleiman Reis, Rejeb Reis, and several of the men, died a martyr's death. Many more were wounded and the ships terribly battered by the cannonballs. At last night put a stop to the fight. One boat was wrecked off the Persian coast, part of the crew escaped, the rest were taken prisoners by the Infidels, and the boat itself captured.

When all this sad news reached the capital, towards the end of Zilhija of the said year 960 (1552), the author of these pages was appointed Admiral of the Egyptian fleet.

I, humble Sidi Ali bin Hūsein, also known as Kiatibi-Rumi (the writer of the West, i. e. of Turkey), most gladly accepted the post. I had always been very fond of the sea, had taken part in the expedition against Rhodes under the Sultan (Suleiman), and had since had a share in almost all engagements, both by land and by sea. I had fought under Khaireddin Pasha, Sinan Pasha, and other captains, and had cruised about on the Western (Mediterranean) sea, so that I knew every nook and corner of it. I had written several books on astronomy, nautical science, and other matters bearing upon navigation. My father and grandfather, since the conquest of Constantinople, had had charge of the arsenal [1] at Galata; they had both been eminent in their profession and their skill had come down to me as an heirloom.

The post now entrusted to me, was much to my taste and I started from Aleppo for Basrah, on the first of Moharram of the year 961 (7 Dec. 1553). I crossed the Euphrates at Biredjik and when in Reka (i. e. Orfah), I undertook a pilgrimage to the

[1] The word here used is the old and correct one, Dar-es-sena (the house of technics), from which word the present *Tersane*, i. e. Arsenal, has originated.

tomb of Abraham, having visited on the way between Nisebin and Mossul the holy graves of the prophets Yunis and Djerdjis and of the sheikh's Mohammed Garabili, Feth Mosuli and Kazib-elban-Mosuli. On the way to Bagdad I made a little detour from Tekrit to Samira, and visited the graves of Iman Ali-el-Hadi and Iman Haman Askeri, after which I came past the towns of Ashik[1] and Maashuk, and through Harbi, past the castle of Semke, on to Bagdad. We crossed the Tigris near Djisr (?) and, after visiting the graves of the saints[2] there, I continued my journey past the fortress of Tëir, to Bire, and crossing the Euphrates near the little town of Masib, I reached Kerbela (Azwie), where I made a pilgrimage to the graves of the martyrs Hasan and Husein. Turning into the steppe near Shefata, I reached Nedjef (Haira) on the second day, and visited the graves of Adam, Noah, Shimun and Ali, and from there proceeded to Kufa, where I saw the mosque with the pulpit under which the prophets

[1] Ashik is now a ruin opposite Samira.

[2] These are: Joshua the prophet, Imam Hambali, Imam Yussuf, Imam Mohammed, Imam Mohammed Ghazali, Ais bin Ishak, Imam Musa Kiazim. Further the Imams: Mohammed Taki, Kamber Ali, Sheikh Abdul Kadir Ghilani, Djuneid Bagdadi, Maaruf Kerkhi, Sheikh Shibli, Seri' Sakati, Haladj Mansur, Beshr-Hafi, Djumerd-Kassab, Behlul Divane, Fazil-bin-Ayaz, Sheikh Shahab-ed-din Sohraverdi, and Sheikh Daud Tagi.

of the house of Ali are buried, and the tombs of Kamber and Duldul. Arrived at the fortress of Hasinia, I visited the grave of the prophet Zilkefl, the son of Aaron, and in Hilla I made pilgrimages to the graves of Iman Mohammed Mehdi and Iman Akil, brother of Ali, and also visited there the mosque of Shem. Again crossing the Euphrates, (this time by a bridge), I resumed my journey to Bagdad and went from there by ship to Basrah. On the way we touched Medain, saw the grave of Selmas Faris, admired Tak Kesri and the castle of Shah Zenan, and went past Imare Bugazi, on the road of Vasit to Zekya, past the strongholds of Adjul and Misra to Sadi-es Sueiba and on to Basrah, where I arrived towards the end of Safar of the said year (beginning of February 1554).

III.

About what happened in Basrah.

On the day after my arrival I had an interview with Mustafa Pasha, who, after seeing my credentials, made over to me the 15 galleys which were needing a great deal of repair. As far as could be, they were put in order, calked and provided with guns which, however, were not to be had in sufficient quantity either from the stores there or from Ormuz. A water supply had also to be arranged for, and as it was yet five months before the time of the monsoon [1], I had plenty of leisure to visit the mosque of Ali and the graves of Hasan Basri, Talha, Zobëir, Uns-bin-Malik, Abdurrahman-bin-Anf, and several martyrs and companions of the Prophet. One night I dreamed that I lost my sword, and as I remembered that a similar thing had happened to Sheikh Muhieddin and had resulted in a defeat, I became greatly alarmed, and, just as I was about to pray to the Almighty for the victory of the Islam arms, I awoke. I kept this dream a secret, but it troubled me for a long time, and when later on Mustafa Pasha sent a detachment of soldiers to take the island of Huweiza, (in which expedition I took part with five of my galleys), and the undertaking resulted in our losing about 100 men all through the fickleness of the Egyptian troops, I fully believed this to be the fulfilment of my dream. But alas! there was more to follow, — for:

> What is decreed must come to pass,
> No matter, whether you are joyful or anxious.

When at last the time of the Monsoon came, the

[1] Mowsim Zemani, literally: "the time of the season." From the Arab. word 'Mowsim' the English 'Monsoon' has orginated.

Pasha sent a trusty sailor with a frigate to Ormuz, to explore the neighbourhood. After cruising about for a month he returned with the news that, except for 4 boats, there was no sign of any ships of the Infidels in those waters. The troops therefore embarked and we started for Egypt.

IV.

What took place in the Sea of Ormuz.

On the first of Shavvāl we left the harbour of Basrah accompanied, as far as Ormuz, by the frigate of Sherifi Pasha. We visited on the way from Mehzari, the grave of Khidr, and proceeding along the coast of Duspul (Dizful), and Shushter in Charik, I made pilgrimages to the graves of Imam Mohammed, Hanifi, and other saints.

From the harbour in the province of Shiraz we visited Rishehr (Bushir?) and after reconnoitring the coasts and unable to get any clue as to the whereabouts of the enemy by means of the Tshekleva[1], I proceeded to Katif situated near Lahsa[2] and Hadjar on the Arabian coast. Unable to learn anything

[1] A small vessel, worked by sails and oars, for the carrying of freights, also called Sacoléve.

[2] Lahsa and Katif, islands in the Persian Gulf, which, together with Ormuz, Bahrein and Kalhata, were famous in the Middle Ages, as stapletowns for the commerce between Persia and India.

there, I went on to Bahrein, where I interviewed the commander of the place, Reis Murad. But neither could he give me any information about the fleet of the Infidels. There is a curious custom at Bahrein. The sailors provided with a leather sack, dive down into the sea and bring the fresh water from the bottom for Reis Murad's use. This water is particularly pleasant and cold in the spring time, and Reis Murad gave me some. God's power is boundless! This custom is the origin of the proverb: "Maradj ŭl bahreia jaltakian," and hence also the name Bahrein.

Next we came to Kis, i. e. old Ormuz, and Barhata and several other small islands in the Green Sea, i. e. the waters of Ormuz, but nowhere could we get any news of the fleet. So we dismissed the vessel, which Mustaffa Pasha had sent as an escort, with the message that Ormuz was safely passed. We proceeded by the coasts of Djilgar and Djadi, past the towns of Keimzar or Leïme, and forty days after our departure, i. e. on the 10th of Ramazan, in the forenoon, we suddenly saw coming towards us the Christian fleet, consisting of four large ships, three galleons, six Portuguese guard ships and twelve galleys (Kalita), 25 vessels in all. I immediately ordered the canopy[1] to be taken down, the anchor

[1] Tentalări fora etmek: tenta تنته the canopy erected to ward

weighed, the guns in readiness, and then trusting to the help of the Almighty, we fastened the filandra [1] to the mainmast, the flags were unfurled and full of courage and calling upon Allah, we commenced to fight. The volley from the guns and cannon was tremendous, and with God's help we sank and utterly destroyed one of the enemy's galleons.

Never before within the annals of history has such a battle been fought, and words fail me to describe it.

The battle continued till sunset, and only then the Admiral of the Infidel fleet, began to show some signs of fear. He ordered the signal gun to fire a retreat, and the fleet turned in the direction of Ormuz [2].

With the help of Allah and under the lucky star of the Padishah the enemies of Islam had been defeated. Night came at last; we were becalmed for awhile, then the wind rose, the sails were set and as the shore was near .... until daybreak [3].

off the rays of the sun. According to *Lehchei-i-Osmani*, a Turkish Dictionary by *Ahmed Vefik Pasha*, Stambul 1293 (1876) the word تنته is translated by chadir, shemsiye, Talal = roof against the rain.

1 Fillandra, according to L. O. a small ensign hoisted on the top of the mainmast.

2 In the text پوچه‌لاتمق pochalatmak (from the Ital. poccia = the right side of a ship), = steering a vessel to the right so as to run before the wind.

3 يايراقدن قوللانوب وقيبى لر دوكوب كيتدكجه كورفز

The next day we continued our previous course. On the day after we passed *Khorfakan*[1] where we took in water, and soon after reached Oman, or rather Sohar[2]. Thus we cruised about for nearly 17 days. When on the 6th of Ramazan, i. e. the day of Kadr-Ghedjesi, a night in the month of Ramazan, we arrived in the vicinity of Maskat and Kalhat[3], we saw in the morning, issuing from the harbour of Maskat, 12 large boats and 22 gŭrabs, 32 vessels in all, commanded by Captain Kuvva[4] the son of the Governor[5]. They carried a large number of troops.

The boats and galleons obscured the horizon with their mizzen sails (Magistra)[6] and Peneta (small sails)

زیاده صاغنقلر دوشوب Japrakdan Kollanub ve Kiglar döküb, git-dikche körfez pa-Kilib ziyade saginiklar Döshüb — is not clear to me, for the literal translation: "which continued along the shore .... until the bay was cleared and much transient rain had fallen" — has no sense.

[1] Khorfekan a place on the eastcoast of Oman, between Ras Dibba and Fedzna.

[2] Sohar also on the eastcoast of Oman.

[3] This is the same as Calatu mentioned by Marco Polo, see: Travels of Marco Polo, by Col. H. Yule. Vol. II, p. 381.

[4] Kuva, Kuvva كوّا appears to me to be really the name of the town Goa, the headquarters of the Portuguese in India.

[5] In the text غورناتور Gornator, Governator.

[6] According to Bianchi, 'voile d'artimon'. The following passage is, owing partly to the defective text, partly to the strange naval technical expressions, unclear and unintelligible.

all set; the guardships spread their round sails (Chember-yelken), and gay with bunting they advanced towards us. Full of confidence in God's protection we awaited them. Their boats attacked our galleys, the battle raged, cannon and guns, arrows and swords made terrible slaughter on both sides. The Badjoalushka (?) penetrated the boats and the Shaikas [1] and tore large holes in their hulls, while our galleys were riddled through by the javelins (Darda) [2] thrown down upon us from the enemy's turrets, which gave them the appearance of bristling porcupines; and they showered down upon us .... [3].

The stones which they threw at us, created quite a whirlpool [4] as they fell into the sea.

One of our galleys was set on fire by a bomb, but strange to say the boat from which it issued shared the like fate. God is merciful! Five of our galleys and as many of the enemy's boats were sunk and utterly wrecked, one of theirs went to the bottom with all sails set. In a word, there was great loss on both sides; our rowers were

[1] Shaika شايقه accord. to L. O. Kazak Kayugi = a Kirghiz boat. Compare the Hungarian Sajka = barge, boat.

[2] Compare the Hungarian d'arda = spear, lance.

[3] In the text: auĕ kajasĭn jagmur اوچ قياسن يغمور = a shower alike the fist of men.

[4] دوكندى Dŏkŭnti, according to L. O., a whirlwind or whirlpool.

now insufficient in number to manage the oars, while running against the current [1] and to fire the cannon [2]. We were compelled to drop anchor (at the stern) and to continue to fight as best we might. The boats had also to be abandoned.

Alemshah Reis, Kara Mustafa, and Kalfat Memi, Captains of some of the foundered ships and Derzi Mustafa Bey the Serdar of the volunteers, with the remainder of the Egyptian soldiers and 200 carpenters (?) had landed on the Arabian shore, and as the rowers were Arabs they had been hospitably treated by the Arabs of Nedjd.

The ships (gurabs) of the Infidel fleet had likewise taken on board the crews of their sunken vessels, and as there were Arabs amongst them, they also had found shelter on the Arabian coast. God is our witness. Even in the war between Khaiveddin Pasha and Andreas Doria [3] no such naval action as this has ever taken place.

When night came, and we were approaching the

1 سیا ایتمك sija Etmk. Incorrectly written in the text as سی ایتمك Accord. to L. O. this word is of Italian Origin, and means to row backwards (?).

2 طوپ صالیا ایتمك top Salia etmek, obselete form of speech.

3 In the text after Andreas Doria (in parentheses) are the words, جند دال *Jend dal*, perhaps a distortion of the Italian *gēnerale* . . . . . ?

bay of Ormuz, the wind began to rise. The boats had already cast two *Lenguvurta* i. e. large anchors [1], the Lushtas (?) were tightly secured and towing the conquered gurabs along we neared the shore while the galleys, dragging their anchors, followed. However, we were not allowed to touch the shore and had to set sail again. During that night we drifted away from the Arabian coast, into the open sea, and finally reached the coasts of Djash [2] in the province of Kerman. This is a long coast but we could find no harbour, and we roamed about for two days before we came to *Kichi Mekran* [3].

As the evening was far advanced we could not land immediately but had to spend another night at sea. In the morning a dry wind carried off many of the crew, and at last, after unheard of troubles and difficulties, we approached the harbour of Sheba [4].

Here we came upon a Notak, i. e. a Brigantine

[1] Of this expression only the word longa (lenga) can be identified with the Italian.

[2] In the text جاشن Djash, more correctly Jask, a harbourtown in Persia, in the vicinity of Belutchistan.

[3] *Rectius:* Kidj-Mekran (Marco Polo's Kesmacoran), as Yule rightly observes, situated on the coast of that part of Kerman, then belonging to India. See: Travels of Marco Polo, by Col. H. Yule. II, p. 335.

[4] In the text شهبا, but on our modern maps (see G. Curzon's map of Persia) given as Shabar, which is the name of the bay as well as of the place.

(Pirate-ship), laden with spoils, and when the watchman sighted us, they hailed us. We told them that we were musulmans, whereupon their captain came on board our vessel; he kindly supplied us with water for we had not a drop left, and thus our exhausted soldiers were invigorated. This was on Bairam day, and for us, as we had now got water, a double feastday. Escorted by the said captain we entered the harbour of Guador [1]. The people there were Beluchistani's and their chief was Malik Djelaleddin, the son of Malik Dinar. The Governor of Guador came on board our ship and assured us of his unalterable devotion to our glorious Padishah. He promised that henceforth, if at any time our fleet should come to Ormuz he would undertake to send 50 or 60 boats to supply us with provisions, and in every possible way to be of service to us. We wrote a letter to the native Prince Djelaleddin to ask for a pilot, upon which a firstclass pilot was sent us, with the assurance that he was thoroughly trustworthy and entirely devoted to the interests of our Padishah.

[1] Guador on the westcoast of Beluchistan, belonging to the Indian Empire.

V.

What we suffered in the Indian Ocean.

God is merciful! With a favorable wind we left the port of Guador and again steered for Yemen. We had been at sea for several days and had arrived nearly opposite to Zofar [1] and Shar, when suddenly from the west arose a great storm known as *fil Tofani* [2]. We were driven back, but were unable to set the sails not even the trinquetla (stormsail). The tempest raged with increasing fury. As compared to these awful tempests the foul weather in the western seas is mere child's play, and their towering billows are as drops of water compared to those of the Indian sea. Night and day were both alike, and because of the frailty of our craft all ballast had to be thrown overboard. In this frightful predicament our only consolation was our unwavering trust in the power of the Almighty. For ten days the storm raged continuously and the rain came down in torrents. We never once saw the blue sky [3].

[1] Zofar ظفار or Dhofar, to the east of Shar. In the middle ages there was a city of that name as mentioned by Marco Polo and Ibn Batuta. See: Travels of M. P., by H. Yule II, p. 380.

[2] Literally: Elephant's flood.

[3] Anabaylik انابايلق means in the vernacular both sun and sky, or more correctly blue sky.

I did all I could to encourage and cheer my companions, and advised them above all things to be brave [1], and never to doubt but that all would end well. A welcome diversion occurred in the appearance of a fish about the size of two galleylengths, or more perhaps, which the pilot declared to be a good omen.

The tide being very strong here and the ebb slow, we had an opportunity of seeing many seamonsters in the neighbourhood of the bay of Djugd, seahorses, large sea serpents, turtles in great quantities, and eels.

The colour of the water suddenly changed to pure white, and at sight of it the pilot broke forth into loud lamentations; he declared we were approaching whirlpools and eddies. These are no myth here; it is generally believed that they are only found on the coasts of Abyssinia and in the neighbourhood of Sind in the bay of Djugd, and hardly ever a ship has been known to escape their fury. So, at least, we are told in nautical books. We took frequent soundings, and when we struck a depth of five Kuladj (= armlengths) the mizzen sails (Orta Yelken) were set, the bowspreat.... [2]

[1] In the text suguria سوغوريه appears to be a word derived from the Italian or the Portuguese.

[2] Here follow some nautical expressions such as ايسه ايليبوب

and .... healing over to the left side, and flying the commander's [1] flag, we drifted about all night and all day until at last in Gods mercy the water rose, the storm somewhat abated and the ship veered right round [2].

The next morning we slackened speed [3] and drew in the sails. A stalward cabin boy [4] (or sailor) was tied to the Djondu (?), whereby the post [5] at the foot of the mizzenmast was weighted down, and the sailrope slightly raised. Taking a survey of our surroundings we caught sight of an Idol-Temple on the coast of Djamher [6]. The sails were drawn in a little more; we passed Formyan and Menglir [7], and directing our course towards Somenat [8], we

isa eyleyub, دورویه اورمق Duruya vurmak, which I do not understand.

1 According to L. O. the Commander's flag.

2 In the text پوپه پرووا popa prova, two words derived from the Italian.

3 ماینه ایتمک maina etmek. Acc. to L. O. the opposite of *fuora et*, therefore to slacken.

4 Direk Nefti = Mastpich, appears to be an expression or epithet for a cabin boy.

5 In the text قازی kazi = a peg or a nail.

6 Rectius Djamkher, a subdivision of Ahmed-nagar, in the Residency of Bombay, (Gazetteer of India VII, p. 127).

7 Perhaps meant for Manglaus, Menglaur, in the District of Sahranpur.

8 سومنات Somenat Somnath, a town in the south of the peninsula of Kathiawar, also the name of the District.

past by that place also. Finally we came to Div [1], but for fear of the unbelievers which dwell there we further drew in our sails and continued in our course with serderma (سردرمه)?

Meanwhile the wind had risen again, and as the men had no control over the rudder, large handles [2] had to be affixed with long double ropes fastened to them. Each rope was taken hold off by four men, and so with great exertion they managed to control the rudder.

No one could keep on his feet on deck [3], so of course it was impossible to walk across [4]. The noise of the .... [5] and the .... [6] was deafening, we could not hear our own voices. The only means of communication with the sailors was by inarticulate words [7], and neither Captain nor Boatswain could

[1] More correctly Diu, an island belonging to the Portuguese in West India, separated from Kathiawar by a narrow stroke of land, with about 13.000 Inhabitants, and politically under Goa. (See: Imperial Gazetteer of India. IV, p. 305).

[2] يكه Yeke, Translated in the L. O. by Dümen Koli = handle of the rudder.

[3] In the text قاردينه Kardina, perhaps more correctly gardina, from the Ital. guarda, watch.

[4] In the text باشدن ياكه bashdan jaña = from side to side.

[5] In the text چارميخ charmikh = cross, cross-beam.

[6] In the text كوميلرن سلسرهسى gumĕlerin selseresi, are unintelligible words, not to be found in any Lexicon.

[7] مانى مانى Mani, mani, acc. to L. O. inarticulate songs, also words.

for a single instant leave their post[1]. The ammunition[2] was secured in the storeroom (.....), and after cutting the ....[3] from the ....[4] we continued our way.

It was truly a terrible day, but at last we reached Gujarat in India, which part of it, however, we knew not, when the pilot suddenly exclaimed: "On your guard! a whirlpool[5] in front!" Quickly the anchors were lowered[6] but the ship was dragged down[7] with great force and nearly submerged. The rowers had left their seats[8] the panic-stricken crew threw off their clothes and clinging some to casks and some to jacks, had taken leave of one another. I also stripped entirely gave my slaves their liberty,

1 In the text قامارتن Kamartan, perhaps from the Ital. camaretta.

2 ايلقاجى aylikchi or aylakchi? both unknown terms but from the context might mean 'in the storeroom'.

3 دون اغاج ton agatsch.

4 تلاز Acc. to L. O. تالاز talaz = waves, from the Greek, but what can possibly be the meaning of talaz Gemisi?

5 دوكندى with چتلاق an expression signifying whirlpool, or more correctly a crevice (cleft), according to L. O. اينجه ياروق indze jaruk = narrow cleft.

6 فونده ايتمك funda etmek (from Ital) throwing the anchor.

7 خرپوشته Kharpushte. in L. O. translated by مقاصلو طام makasli tam, deck?

8 قدينه Kadina, perhaps catena = chains, fetters, as the rowers in those days were generally slaves.

and vowed to give 100 florins [1] to the poor of Mecca.

Presently one of the anchors broke from its crook and another at the podjuz [2]; two more were lost, the ship gave a terrible jerk — and in another instant we were clear of the breakers. The pilot declared that had we been wrecked off Fisht-Kidsur, a place between Diu and Daman [3], nothing could have saved us. Once more the sails were set, and we decided to make for the Infidel coast; but after duly taking note of tide and current, and having made a careful study of the chart [4], I came to the conclusion that we could not be very far off the mainland. I consulted the Horoscope in the Koran, and this also counselled patience. So we commenced to examine the hold of the ship and found that the storeroom was submerged, in some places up to the walls, in some places higher still. We had shipped much water and all hands set to work at once to bale it out. In one or two places the bottom [5] had

[1] In the text فلوری filūri, from the Ital. fiori = a gold-coin.

[2] پوحوز podjuz?

[3] Daman, a Portuguese possession in the bay of Cambay, with about 50.000 Inhabitants; was pillaged first in the year 1531, and retaken in 1553.

[4] In the text خارتی‌دن کرته ریز ایتمك Kharitadin Kerte riz etmek, i. e. studying the strokes and lines of the compass.

[5] In the text کوك Kŏk = root, lower part of a body.

to be ripped up to find the outlet [1] so as to reduce the water.

Towards afternoon the weather had cleared a little, and we found ourselves about two miles off the port of Daman in Gujarat in India. The other ships had already arrived, but some of the galleys were waterlogged not far from the shore, and they had thrown overboard, oars, boats, and casks, all which wreckage eventually was borne ashore by the rapidly rising tide. We were obliged to lie to for another five days and five nights, exposed to a strong spring-tide, accompanied by floods of rain; for we were now in the Badzad [2] or rainy season of India, and there was nothing for it but to submit to our fate. During all this time, we never once saw the sun by day, nor the stars by night; we could neither use our clock nor our compass and all on board anticipated the worst. It seems a miracle that of the three ships lying there, thrown on their sides, the whole crew eventually got safely to land.

[1] In the text فاليا falia, according to L. O. from the Italian and meaning touch-hole.

[2] Compare the Persian بادزد badzed = whirlwind, tempest; more correctly gust of wind from Bad = Wind and Zeden = to strike.

VI.

What happened in the Province of Gujarat.

After five days, in God's mercy, the wind somewhat abated[1]. All that was saved of the wreckage, cannon and other armament we left with the Governor of Daman, Malik Esed, who, since the time of Sultan Ahmed, the ruler of Gujarat, had held office there. In the harbour were some Djonk's[2] i. e. Monsoon ships belonging to Samiri, the ruler of Calcutta. The captains came on board our ship and assured us of the devotion of their chief to the Padishah. They brought us a letter which said that Samiri was waging war day and night against the Portuguese Infidels and that he was expecting the arrival of an Imperial fleet from Egypt under the guidance of the pilot Ali, which was to put the Portuguese to flight. Melik Esed, the Governor, gave me to understand that the fleet of the Infidels was on its

[1] In the text بوناتسه ایدوب bunatsa ediib, described by the author to mean bashkoyub = to lie down. What is the origin and meaning of Bunatza I am unable to say.

[2] In the text جونك Djonk = a large ship, used principally in China. First mentioned by the Monk Odorico di Pordenone in 1331. See: Glossary of Anglo-Indian words, by Yule and Burnell. p. 360.

way, that it behoved us to avoid it and if possible to reach the fortress of Surat. This news frightened the crew. Some of them immediately took service under Melik Esed, and some went ashore in the boats and proceeded by land to Surat.

I remained on board with a few faithful of the men, and after procuring a Dindjuy [1], or pilotboat for each vessel, we set out for the harbour of Surat. After great difficulties we reached the open. Presently the Kutwal [2], Aga Hamsa, hailed us with a letter from Umad-el-mulk, the Grand Vizier of Sultan Ahmed, who informed us that there were large numbers of Infidels about, and that Daman being a free port we had better be careful. He would allow us to come to Surat if we liked, as we were now in most perilous waters. This was exactly what we wanted to do, so we struggled on for five days longer [3] sailing at the flow, riding at anchor at the ebb of the tide, until at last we reached the harbour

[1] Compare Dingy, Dinghy (see: Glossary of Anglo-Indian Colloquial Words and Phrases, page 245). Literally the name of a ship or large boat, on the coast of Mekran; the word is also known in English but it originates from Beluchistan correctly speaking it means a pilotship.

[2] Kotwal, kutwal = commander of a fortress, also policeman. Of Turkish origin, from the word küt = to guard, to watch, would be more correctly, küteöl = guardian.

[3] In the text خورقاريده Khurkaride, is unknown to me.

of Surat, fully three months after our departure from Basrah.

Great was the joy of the mohammedans at Surat when they saw us come; they hailed us as their deliverers (lit. Khidr) and said: "You have come to Gujarat in troublous times; never since the days of Noah has there been a flood like unto this last, but neither is it within the memory of man, that a ship from Rum (Turkey) has landed on these coasts. We fervently hoped that God in his mercy would soon send an Ottoman fleet to Gujarat, to save this land for the Ottoman empire and to deliver us from the Indian unbelievers."

The cause of the disturbances was this: After the death of Sultan Bahadur, the ruler of Gujarat, one of his relatives, a youth of twelve years old, had succeeded to the throne. The army had acknowledged him, but one of the nobles, Nasir-ul-Mulk, had refused to take the oath of allegiance, and had raised the banner of sovereignty on his own behalf [1]. He had many adherents, took the stronghold of Burudj [2], left a sufficient garrison to keep it, proceeded himself

[1] Cheter Kaldirmak چتر قالدرمق means literally, to raise the Sunshade (umbrella), this being the symbol of sovereignty in India.

[2] More correctly Broatsh, a place north-west of Surat in the province of Gujarat on the right bank of the Nerbudda. This place has from time immemorial belonged to the Moslem rulers of Ahmedabad and has twice been pillaged by the Portuguese (in 1536 and 1546).

to another town, and then called in the aid of the Governor of the Infidels (Portuguese) at Goa, promising that in return for his services the harbours [1] on the coast of Gujarat, viz. Daman, Surat, Burudj, Ketbaye, Sumenat, Minglur, and Furmeyan, should be thrown open to the Portuguese, while he would retire to the land of the interior.

Sultan Ahmed had immediately collected an army to go to Burudj, and when informed of our arrival he took from our troops 200 gunners and other men, and advanced towards Burudj. On the third day we who were left behind, were attacked by the Infidel captains of Goa, Diu, Shiyul, Besai, and the Provador [2]; five in all, commanding 7 large galleons and 80 gurabs. We went ashore, pitched our tents and threw up entrenchments; for two whole months we were busy preparing for battle. But the tyrant Nasir-ul-Mulk, who had joined with the Infidels, had hired murderers to kill me; they were however discovered by the guard and fled. Again another time he tried to poison my food, but being warned by the Kutwal of Surat this attempt to take my life also failed. Meanwhile Sultan Ahmed had taken the stronghold of Burudj and sent

[1] In the text: benadir, Arab. Plural of the Persian word بندر bender = harbour.

[2] In the text پرواذور Provador, circumscribed as meaning دریا قپودانی derya Kapudani = Admiral.

two of his officers, Khudavend and Djihanghir, with elephants and troops to Surat, while he proceeded to Ahmedabad, where a youth, called Ahmed, a relation of Sultan Ahmed, had in the meantime raised a revolt. A battle followed in which the usurper was wounded, Hasan Khan, one of his adherents, killed, and his army put to flight. Sultan Ahmed reascended his throne and as Nasir-ul-Mulk died of vexation over his misfortunes, peace was once more restored in Gujarat.

When the Infidels heard of this they sent an Envoy to Khudavend Khan to say that they did not mind so much about Surat but that their hostility was chiefly directed towards the Admiral of Egypt, viz. my humble person. They demanded that I should be given up to them, but were refused, and my soldiers would have killed the Envoy but I reminded them that we were on foreign soil and must commit no rash deeds. It so happened that a runaway Infidel gunner from one of my ships had enlisted on the ship of the Envoy, and, knowing a good deal about our affairs, he had undertaken to prevent our departure after the holiday of Kurban. No sooner had this come to the knowledge of my men, then they attacked the Envoy's ship and captured the Infidel who was executed on the spot, greatly to the alarm of the Envoy.

There is in Gujarat a tree of the palm-tribe, called tari agadji (millet tree). From its branches cups are suspended and when the cut end of a branch is placed into one of these vessels, a sweet liquid, something of the nature of arrack, flows out in a continuous stream; and this fluid, by exposure to the heat of the sun, presently changes into a most wonderful wine. Therefore at the foot of all such trees drinking booths have been placed, which are a great attraction to the soldiers. Some of my men, having indulged in the forbidden drink, determined to kill their Serdar. One of these profligates, Yagmur by name, one evening after sunset surprised Hussain Aga the Serdar of the Circassians. A few comrades rushed to his assistance, there was some fighting and two young men were wounded, but one, Hadji Memi, was killed. Then the soldiers pressed round, and implored me to punish the evil-doers, but I again reminded them that we were on foreign soil, in the land of a foreign Padishah, and that our laws had no force here. "What", they cried, "the laws of our Padishah hold good everywhere. You are our Admiral, judge according to our law, and we will be the executioners!" Thereupon I pronounced judgment according to the law of the Koran, which says: "Eye for eye, life for life, nose for nose, ear for ear, etc."

The man was executed, and peace restored. When

the nobles of the Begs heard of the occurence, they took the lesson to heart, and the Envoy immediately hired a conveyance and went to Sultan Ahmed.

But my troops were getting dissatisfied. In Surat, Khudavend Khan had been paying them from 50 to 60 paras per day, and in Burudj, Adil Khan had done the same. At last their pent-up feelings burst forth and they argued as follows: "It is now nearly two years since we have received any pay, our goods are lost and the ships dismantled; the hulks are old, and our return to Egypt is practically made impossible." The end was that the greater part of them took service in Gujarat.

The deserted ships with all their tools and implements were given over to Khudavend Khan, under condition that he should immediately remit to the Sublime Porte, the price agreed upon for the sale.

After receiving a confirmatory note to this effect, both from Khudavend Khan and Adil Khan, I started on my journey to Ahmedabad[1] in the beginning of Muharram of the year 962 (End of November 1552), accompanied by Mustafa Aga, the Ketkhuda (chief officer) of the Egyptian Janissaries, and Ali Aga, the Captain of the gunners (both of which had remained faithful to their Padishah), and

[1] Ahmedabad, the chief town of the Province of that name, 310 Engl. miles north of Bombay.

with about 50 men. A few days took us from Burudj to Belodra [1], and from there we proceeded to Champanir [2].

On our way we saw some very curious trees, whose crowns reached up to the sky, and the branches swarmed with bats of such extraordinary size that their wings on the stretch measured 40 inches across. The most curious part about the trees, however, was that the roots hung down from the branches and when touching the ground, planted themselves and produced new trees. Thus from one tree, from 10 to 20 new ones sprung up. The name of this tree is the Tobi tree [3], and more then a thousand (?) people can find shelter under their shade. Besides these we saw several Zokum trees [4]. Parrots were very plentiful and as for the monkeys, thousands of them made their appearance in our camp every evening. They carried their young in their arms, made the most ridiculous grimaces and strongly brought to our minds the stories of Djihan Shah, according to whom these animals live in a community but acknowledge no

[1] More correctly Balotra, a town in Jodpur (Radjhputana).

[2] Champanir, a mountain fortress in Gujarat in the Province of Pendj-Mahal, 250 Engl. miles north-east of Bombay.

[3] Compare Tuba-tree, with the Sidra-trees of the Mohammedan Paradise.

[4] Zokum زقوم a tree which acc. to the Koran grows only in Hell. Its fruit resembles the Plantain and serves as food for the condemned.

head among them. At nightfall they always retired to their own place.

After a great many vicissitudes we at last arrived in Mahmudabad[1], and after a journey of 50 days in Ahmedabad the Capital of Gujarat. There I visited the Sultan, his Grand Vizier Imad-ul-Mulk, and other dignitaries. The Sultan, to whom I presented my credentials, was pleased to receive me most graciously and he assured me of his devotion to our glorious Padishah. He gave me a horse, a team of camels[2] and money for the journey.

At Cherkes, in the vicinity of Ahmedabad, is the grave of Sheikh Ahmed Magrebi, which I visited. One day, being at the house of Imad-ŭl-Mŭlk, I met the Infidel Envoy, and our host addressed him in this way, "We have need of the Sultan of Turkey. Our ships touch the ports of his Empire, and if we were not free to do so, it would be bad for us. Moreover he is the Padishah of the Islamitic world, and it is not seemly that we should be expected to deliver up his Admiral to you." I became very angry at this speech and cried: "Hold, thou cursed tongue!" Thou foundest me with a shattered fleet, but

[1] At present there is only a place of that name known in Oudh. but not in Gujarat.

[2] Bir Katar deve = a team of camels. Katar = team, means ten camels.

I swear by God Almighty, thou shalt see ere long not only Ormuz but Goa itself, yield before the victorious arms of the great Padishah [1]!" To which the unbeliever made the following answer: "Henceforth not so much as a bird will be able to leave the ports of India." I replied: "One need not necessarily go by water, there is a landroute also." He was silent after that and the subject was dropped.

A few days after this Sultan Ahmed offered me the command of the Province of Burudj, with a very large income, but I refused, saying that I would not stay if he gave me the whole of the land. One night in my dream I saw the Khalifa Murteza Ali. I had a piece of paper before me with Ali's seal upon it. With this seal, the seal of God to help me, away with all fear, for in its strength all foreign waters were mine to command.

Next morning I told my dream to my companions and all were glad with me. I asked for permission to depart, and the ruler granted my request out of respect for our Padishah.

[1] Very characteristic is the piece of poetry here introduced. It is probably a Turkish sea-song of that time. It says:

We roam the waters far and wide,
And bring confusion upon our enemies;
Revenge and hatred is our Motto,
For we are Khairreddin's [a]) troops.

[a]) Khaireddin Pasha, Suleiman's renowned Admiral known in Europe as Barbarossa.

Amongst the learned [1] of this land of Banians [2], there is a tribe which they call the *Bats*, whose business it is to escort merchants or travellers from one land into another, and for a very small renumeration, they guarantee their perfect safety. Should the Rajputs [3], i. e. the mounted troops of the land, attack the caravan, the Bats point their daggers at their own breast, and threaten to kill themselves if they should presume to do the slightest harm to the travellers entrusted to their care. And out of respect for the Bats, the Rajputs generally desist from their evil purpose, and the travellers proceed on their way unmolested. Occasionally however, the Bats carry out their threat, otherwise it would have no force. But if such a thing does happen, if a caravan is attacked and the suicide of the Bats becomes necessary, this is considered a terrible calamity, and the superstition of the people demands that the offenders be put to death, and not only the offenders themselves but the chief of the Rajputs deems it necessary to kill their sons and daughters also,

[1] In the text بامي Bami, may possibly be a slip of the pen and intended for Brahmin.

[2] Banians = Indian merchants, more especially from the Province of Gujarat, who from time immemorial have traded with the harbourtowns of Arabia.

[3] Rectus Rajput, a warlike race, probably descended from the Ural-Altaic race.

in fact to exterminate the whole of their race. The Mohammedans of Ahmedabad had given us two such Bats as an escort, and so, about the middle of Safar of the said year, we started on our overland journey to Turkey.

In five days we reached Patna [1], travelling in carriages, and visited the grave of Sheikh Nizam the Pir (spiritual chief) of Patna. Here Shir Khan and his brother Mŭsa Khan had collected an army, to fight Behluj Khan, the ruler of Radanpoor [2]. For fear of our siding with their enemies, the people tried to retain us, and would not allow us to proceed on our journey until the battle should be over. We showed them, however, that we had not come to render either party any assistance, but that we only wanted to continue our journey in peace, and had a pass from their ruler to that effect. Then at last they let us go, and after five days we came to Radanpoor where I was presented to Mahmud Khan, but he treated me very rudely, and insisted on forcibly detaining three of my companions before he would consent to our departure.

[1] This cannot be the town of that name in Bengal, as this lies more to the south and could not be reached from Ahmedabad in five days.

[2] Radhanpur, the capital of the district of that name in the Presidency of Bombay.

On the way we met some friendly Rajputs; their Beg was of great service to us, and gave me a letter of protection (free pass). The camels were hired, and after dismissing the Bats which the people of Ahmedabad had sent with us, we continued our journey.

VII.

What befell us in the Province of Sind.

Leaving on the first of Rebiul-Evvel we came after a ten days journey to Parker [1] a town of the Rajputs. Here we were surprised by the Infidels, but thanks to the letter of protection and a few presents, we were let free; quite anticipating further dangers, however, we were on our guard when next day a band of hostile Rajputs commenced a free fight with us. Immediately I ordered all the camels to be let down on their knees so as to form a ring round us, and then the firing began on all sides. The Infidels, not prepared for this, sent us word that 'they had not come to fight but to exact the passage money,' to which I made reply: "We are not merchants and carry nothing but medicines

[1] More correctly Parkar or Nagar-Parkar, the name of a district and a place in the Presidency of Bombay.

and Mohurs [1] on which we have already paid duty; but if there be anything further to pay we are quite prepared to do so." This had the desired effect, they let us pass, and for about ten days we wandered through deserts and sandy places, until we reached Wanga [2] the frontiertown of Sind. Here we hired fresh camels, and in five days we came to Djoona [3] and Baghi-Feth. The throne of Sind was then occupied by Shah Husein Mirza. He had reigned for 40 years, but during the last 5 years he had become invalided [4] and unable to mount his horse, so now he only went about on board his ship in the river Sihun [5].

At that time Isa Terkhan, the commander of the capital of Sind, called Tata [6], had put to death a number of able officers belonging to Shah Husein, after which he had captured the treasure, stored in

[1] Muhre مهره a stone, which, so says the legend, is found in the head of the serpent and the dragon, and possesses miraculous power. Many Dervishes carry one of these stones in their girdle to trade upon the superstition of the ignorant people.

[2] In the text وانكه. As a town, Wanga is unknown to me, unless it be intended for Wanna, in the district of Cathiawar in the Presidency of Bombay.

[3] More correctly Junaghar, the name of a Province and town in Cathiawar, Presidency of Bombay.

[4] In the text نيم تن = half body viz. ailing.

[5] Sihun, means the Indus.

[6] Tatta (Thats or Nagar Thats) in the District of Caratchi.

the fortress of Nasrabad, and divided it amongst his men, and then proclaimed himself as Humayun Shah. (It says literally that he had this title inserted in the Friday-prayers and ordered the Nakara [1] to be played). Thereupon Shah Husein had nominated his adopted brother Sultan Mahmud as commander of the landtroops, and he himself with 400 ships had set out against the rebels. Hearing of my arrival he received me with great honour. It was then the beginning of the month of Rabia-al-Sani. He gave me festive apparel [2] and conferred upon us the title of a God-sent army [3]; he offered me besides all this the governorship of Bender-Lahuri or Duyuli-Sindi. Of course I refused this offer, but when I requested permission to continue my journey, I was given to understand that I should not be allowed to do so until after the successful termination of the campaign. He also wrote a letter to our glorious Padishah, explaining matters; in a word he did not rest until he had quite cleared us from being mixed up in this war with Isa Khan. The Mohammedans

[1] Nakara نقره band of music was formerly considered in Central Asia as a sign of sovereignty.

[2] Serpay vermek سرپای ویرمك = to distribute festive apparel, is a great mark of distinction in Central Asia, but as the expression is unknown in Turkey, the author has had to circumscribe it.

[3] ادیمز لشکر غیب قویوب = he gave us the name of: a mystic army.

pleaded in vain that our arms could bring no evil upon them [1], for said they, "are we not all of one nation, and are not many of our sons and brethren in the rebel army?" And this was perfectly true. I had an interview with Sheikh Abdŭl Vahab and received his blessing; I also visited the graves of the Sheikh's Djemali and Miri.

The campaign lasted a month, earthworks were thrown up and cannon raised thereon, but as Tata lies on an island and their shot did not reach so far, the fortress could not be taken. Nevertheless there was great loss of life on both sides. At last a compromise was decided upon. Mir Isa relinquished his adherence to Humayun Padishah, returned to his allegiance to Husein Mirza and sent his son Mir Salih with presents of submission. On the other hand Husein Mirza gave the remainder of the treasure, which Mir Isa had divided amongst his troops, to Mir Salih. Isa was reinstated in his former rank, and Mirza sent him a formal acceptance of his allegiance by the hand of the Vizier Molla Yari. He also sent him a Nakara by Tugbeghi, the chief standard-bearer, and released from prison the ten rebels from the tribes of Argun and

[1] Literally: Tüfenklerinizde mühre olmazsūm تفنكلريكزده مهره اولمزسون = there should be no dragonstone, i. e. sorcery in your guns.

Tarkhan [1], which had sided with Mir Isa. Mir Isa, from his side, had sent back the wife of Husein Shah, called Hadji Begum, and in the first days of Djemadi-ul-evvel, Sultan Mahmud returned by land, and Shah Husein by water, to the city of Bakar. On the tenth day after his wife had rejoined him, Shah Husein died, and it was supposed that she had poisoned him.

Directly after his father's death, Sultan Mahmud divided the property in three parts. One part was for the wife of the deceased and another part he sent to Mir Isa by a Khodja. The body was taken to Tata; he lent me one of his own ships, and providing himself with horses, camels, and other necessaries, returned by land to Bakar. While the body of Mirza, with his wife and an escort of 50 ships were on their way to Tata, the soldiers attacked the remaining vessels and plundered them. The sailors took flight, and we, the passengers, were compelled to take command of the ships. Beset on all sides by the Djagatai's (Central Asians), we relinquished our firearms, and barely escaped with our lives. At last, after struggling for ten days against the stream, we made our way to Nasirpur [2].

[1] Argun and Terkhan are two Turkish tribes in Central Asia, direct descendants of the Transoxanian warriors, which came with Baber to India.

[2] Now Nasirabad, the name of several places in Sind.

This town had been plundered by the Radja, i. e. the Bey of the Rajputs.

We were greeted with the news that Mir Isa with 10.000 valiant soldiers was pursuing Sultan Mahmud and that his son, Mir Salih, with 80 ships was close behind us. This was very perplexing but I decided at once to turn back. We prayed long together, and then started on our return to Tata. Three days later we passed Mir Salih in the river. I went on board his ship with a few small presents and he asked me where we were going. I said "We are going to your father," whereupon he told me to go back with him. I said "we have no sailors on board," so he gave me fifteen of his crew, and thus compelled to turn back, we had another weary ten days to get through. One day I chanced upon Mir Isa in a small town of Sind. Here I also found the former partizans of the late Mirza, who were tired of fighting and desired peace. Isa received me with great honour, forgave me the past and allowed me to remain a few days, saying that he intended shortly to send his son Mir Salih to Humayun Padishah, and that I might as well travel under his escort, for, he added "Sultan Mahmud will never allow thee to pass Bakar, he is a son of Ferrukh Mirza and wants to become Padishah." This proposal however did not suit me, and I insisted upon continuing my journey forthwith, suggesting that he should give us back the ships, lately taken from us, and also to send a messenger in advance, for with God's help he, Sultan Mahmud, would probably have to submit to the Padishah (Humayun), and thus peace be restored. Isa agreed to this, and gave me seven ships with their complement of sailors. He wrote to the Padishah to assure him of his unalterable loyalty, and so we went on our way. We were struck with the enormous size of the fish (Alligators?) sporting in the river, as also with the quantities of tigers on the banks. It was necessary to keep up a perpetual warfare with the people of Semtche and Matchi, through whose territory our course lay, and thus we reached Siyawan [1] and shortly after we came to Bukkur by the way of Patri [2] and Dible. Here I fell in with Sultan Mahmud and his Vizier Molla Yari. I offered a small gift to the former, who thereupon expressed his willingness to submit himself to Humayun, and also to make peace with Mir Isa.

I composed a Chronogramm on the death of Husein Mirza and presented Sultan Mahmud with

[1] Perhaps meant for Sehivan in Naushar on the Indus.

[2] Patri, now a station on the railwayline to Bombay, Baroda, and Central India; also the name of a small state belonging to Kathiawar.

two Ghazels [1], after which I requested permission to continue my journey. This was granted, but as the route past Kandahar was made unsafe by the inroads [2] of Sultan Bahadur, a son of Sultan Haidar, the Ozbeg, and as the season of the Semum (hot winds), had now commenced, the Sultan offered to give me an escort by the way of Lahore, warning me to be on my guard against the Djats, a hostile tribe which had its abode there. But whichever route I chose I should have to wait a while yet, and as a matter of fact I waited for a whole month. One night in my dream I saw my mother, who told me that she had seen her highness Fatima in a dream, and had learned from her the glad news, that I should soon be coming home, safe and sound.

When next morning I told this dream to my companions they were full of good courage. Sultan Mahmud, when he heard of it, at once consented to my departure. He gave me a beautiful horse, a

1 Our author, according to the spirit of the age was not only a brave warrior and sailor, but also a poet, using the East-Turkish Dialect (Djagatai). His muse has no special features, and with regard to his choice of words they betray a strong tendency towards the Osmanli dialect. It is nevertheless interesting to note in how short a time he mastered this dialect and that more than 100 years after Baber, the Djagatai tongue maintained itself as the court- and book-language in India. In our translation we necessarily omit these poetic effusions, as irrelevant.

2 Literally: Kazak olmak قازاق اولمق = wandering.

team of camels a large and a small tent [1] and money for the journey. He also provided me with a letter of recommendation to Humayun, and an escort of 250 mounted cameldrivers, from Sind. Thus we departed about the middle of Shaaban and reached the fortress of Mav in five days, travelling by the way of Sultanpoor [2]. As the Djats were very troublesome, we did not take the route of Djenghelistan (the forest), but preferred to go through the steppe. On the second day we came to the spring but found no water, and many of my companions nearly succumbed with heat and thurst. I gave them some Teriak (opium), of the very best quality [3], and on the second day they were recovered. After this experience we deemed it advisable to leave the desert and to return to Mav, for the proverb says truly, 'A stranger is an ignorant man.' In the steppe we saw ants as large as sparrows.

Our escort from Sind was afraid of the wood, and I had to inspire my own people with fresh courage. I placed 10 gunners in front, 10 in the centre and 10 in the rear of our caravan, and thus,

[1] In the text خیمه و شامیانه Kheime we shamiane, the latter being more a kind of large sunshade.

[2] As there are several places called Sultanpoor and Mav, the stations here mentioned are difficult to identify on the map.

[3] تریاق فاروق teriaki faruk = the best quality of Teriak or Opium.

trusting in God's protection, we commenced the journey. The people from Sind also took courage after this, and went with us.

Thus, after manifold dangers, we came after ten days to Utchi [1] or Autchi where I visited Sheikh Ibrahim and received his blessing. I also made a pilgrimage to the graves of the Sheikh's Djemali and Djelali. In the beginning of Ramazan we resumed our journey and came to the river Kara or Kere [2], which we crossed by means of a raft. The people of Sind gave us permission to proceed as far as the Machvara [3] and this river was crossed by boats. On the other side we found 500 Djats awaiting us, but our fire-arms frightened them and they did not attack. We advanced unmolested, and reached the town of Multan on the 15th of Ramazan.

VIII.

My experiences in Hindustan.

In Multan I only visited the graves of the Sheikh's

[1] In Walker's large Map of India, called *Utsch* a small place on the left bank of the Pendtjend, a tributary of the Indus.

[2] On Modern Maps of India it is marked as Gharra, by which name the Sutlej is also known.

[3] On the way from Utch to Multan there is a river called Trimba. But I have not anywhere come upon a river called Machvara.

Baha eddin Zekeria, Rukneddin, and Sadreddin. I received a blessing from Sheikh Mohammed Radjva and, after receiving permission to continue my journey from Sultan Mirmiran Mirza Hasan, we proceeded towards Lahore. In Sadkere I visited Sheikh Hamid, received his blessing, and in the first days of the Month Shawwal, we came to Lahore. The political state of the country was as follows: After the death of Selim Shah a son of Shir Khan, the former Sovereign of Hindustan, Iskender Khan, had come to the throne. When the Padishah Humayun heard this, he immediately left Kabul and marched his army to India, took Lahore, and fought Iskender Khan near Sahrand. He won the battle and took 400 elephants besides several cannon and 400 chariots. Iskender Khan escaped to the fortress of Mankut, and Humayun sent Shah Abul-Maali with a detachment of soldiers after him. Humayun himself proceeded to his residence at Delhi and despatched his officers to different places. The Ozbeg, Iskender Khan, he sent to Agra, and others to Firuzshah Senbel [1], Bayana and Karwitch. War raged on all sides, and when I arrived at Lahore the Governor, Mirza Shah, would not let me continue my journey until I had seen the Padishah (Humayun). After

[1] Rectius Sambal, a place in the District of Muradabad, in the Northeast of India.

sending the latter word of my arrival, he received orders to send me forthwith to Delhi. Meanwhile a whole month had been wasted, but finally we were sent off with an escort. The river Sultanpoor was crossed in boats and after a journey of 20 days we arrived towards the end of Dulkaada, by the route of Firuzshah [1] in the capital of India, called Delhi. As soon as Humayun heard of our arrival, he sent the Khanikhanan [2] and other superior officers with 400 elephants and some thousand men to meet us, and, out of respect and regard for our glorious Padishah, we were accorded a brilliant reception. That same day the Khanikhanan prepared a great banquet in our honour, and as it is the custom in India to give audience in the evening, I was that night introduced with much pomp and ceremony into the Imperial hall. After my presentation I offered the Emperor a small gift, and a chronogramm upon the conquest of India, also two Ghazels, all of which pleased the Padishah greatly. Forthwith I begged for permission to continue my journey, but this was not granted. Instead of that I was offered a Kulur [3] and the governorship over the district of

[1] Also called Firuzpoor, in Penjab.

[2] i. e. Khan of the Khans like the Mirimiran of the Persians, and the Beglerbeghi of the Turks.

[3] Rectius Kurur = 10.000.000 Rupies = one Million Pounds Sterling.

Kharcha[1]. I refused, and again begged to be allowed to go, but for only answer I was told that I must at least remain for one year, to which I replied: "By special command of my glorious Padishah I went by sea to fight the miserable unbelievers. Caught in a terrible hurricane, I was wrecked off the coast of India; but it is now my plain duty to return to render an account to my Padishah, and it is to be hoped that Gujarat will soon be delivered out of the hands of the unbelievers." Upon this Humayun suggested the sending of an envoy to Constantinople to save my going, but this I could not agree to, for it would give the impression that I had purposely arranged it so. I persisted in my entreaties and he finally consented, adding however: "We are now close upon the three months of continuous (Birshegal)[2], i. e. the rainy season. The roads are flooded[3] and impassable, remain therefore till the weather improves. Meanwhile calculate Solar and Lunar Eclipses, their degree of latitude and their exact date in the Calendar. Assist our astrologers in studying the course of the sun, and instruct us concerning the points of the Equator. When all this is done, and the weather

[1] In the text پرکنه خرجه Pergenei Kharcha.

[2] برشکال birshegal, probably a Hindustani word.

[3] In the text Kish = Winter, also bad weather, rainy season. Comp. Kish Kiamet = very foul weather.

should improve before the three months are over, then thou shalt go hence."

All this was said solemnly and decisively. I had no alternative, but must submit to my fate. I took no rest however, but laboured on night and day. At last I had accomplished the astronomical observations, and about the same time Agra fell into the hands of the Padishah. I immediately wrote a chronogramm for the occasion which found much favour. One day, during an audience, the conversation turned upon Sultan Mahmud of Bukkur, and I suggested that some official contract (Ahdnameh = agreement) should be made with him, to which Humayun agreed. The document was drawn up, and the Emperor dipping his fist in saffron pressed it upon the paper, this being the Tughra [1] or Imperial signature. Thereupon the document was sent to Sultan Mahmud.

The Sultan was much pleased and both he and his Vizier Molla Yari expressed their thanks for my intervention in a private letter, which I showed to His Majesty, who had entrusted me with the transaction.

This incident furnished the material for a Ghazel,

[1] Opinions differ as to the exact nature of the Tughra (signature of Turkish rulers: rectius tora = decree). Some say that it is merely a florish, others hold that it is the impression of the hand. In Central Asia, Turkish Monarchs used to dip their hand in blood, hence the expression 'al-tamga' = red seal. The descendants of Baber first introduced into India the use of the yellow dye, saffron.

with which the Sovereign was so delighted that he called me a second Mir Ali Shir [1]. I modestly declined the epithet, saying that it would be presumption on my part to accept such praise, that, on the contrary, I should consider myself fully rewarded to be allowed to gather up the gleanings after him. Whereupon the Sovereign remarked: "If for one more year thou perfectest thyself in this kind of poetry thou wilt altogether supplant Mir Ali Shir in the affections of the people of the Djagatai's." In a word Humayun loaded me with marks of his favour. One day I was talking to Khoshhal, the Imperial archer, and the Sovereign's special confident; a superb youth. He used to take part in the poetical discussions, and provided me with material for two Ghazels which soon became popular all over India and were in everybody's mouth. The same good fortune attended my acquaintance with the Afetabedji [2], Abdurrahman Bey, a courtier who

[1] Mir Ali Shir the greatest poet of the Turks in Central Asia, born, according to Khondemir, in the year 844 (1440) and died in H. 906 (1500). He wrote under the name of *Newai*. His compositions, which are unquestionably superior to any other East Turkish productions, enjoy to this day great popularity amongst the Turks of the interior of Asia.

[2] Afetabe = waterbasin, and Afetabedji = he who holds the waterbasin; a high court dignity in Central Asia, and later on also among the Moguls in India. The former Khans of Khokand had received the title of Afetabedji from the Sultan of Turkey.

also rejoiced in the confidence and affection of the Monarch, and was his constant companion in private life. He also entered the poetical contest, and I composed two Ghazels upon him.

In a word, poetical discussions were the order of the day, and I was constantly in the presence of the Emperor. One day he asked me whether Turkey was larger than India, and I said: "If by Turkey your Majesty means Rum proper, i. e. the province of Siwas [1], then India is decidedly the larger, but if by Turkey you mean all the lands subject to the ruler of Rum, India is not by a tenth part as large." "I mean the entire empire," replied Humayun. "Then," I said, "it appears to me, your Majesty, that the seven regions over which Iskender (i. e. Alexander the Great) had dominion, were identical with the present Empire of the Padishah of Turkey. History records the life and the reign of Iskender, but it is not reasonable to suppose that he actually visited and personally ruled these seven regions, for the inhabited world (the fourth part of the present inhabited world), is 180 degrees longitude and from the equator about 60 degrees latitude. Its area, according to astronomical calculations, covers 1.668.670

[1] Our author means by Siwas the old seat of the Osmans, but in India and in Central Asia, *Rum* is generally understood to stand for the West, and more particularly for the Ottoman Empire.

fersakhes. It is therefore an utter impossibility for any man, to visit and govern all these lands in person. Perhaps he only owned a portion of each of these regions (Iklim), in the same way as the Padishah of Turkey does." "But has the ruler of Turkey possessions in all these regions?" asked Humayun. "Yes certainly," I replied, "the first is Yemen, the second Mecca, the third Egypt, the fourth Aleppo, the fifth Constantinople, the sixth Kaffa and the seventh Ofen and Vienna [1]. In each of these regions the Padishah of Turkey appoints his Beglerbeg and Kadi, who rule and govern in his name. Moreover I was told in Gujarat, by the merchants Khodja Bashi and Kara Hasan (God alone knows whether their story is true), that when the Turkish merchants in China desired to insert the name of their Sovereign in the Bairam prayers on Bairamday, they brought the request before the Khakan of China, stating that their Sovereign was Padishah of Mecca, Medina, and the Kibla (Direction of the prayer), and therefore entitled to have his name inserted in the Bairam prayers. The Khakan, although an unbeliever, had insight enough to see the

[1] As the Turks never conquered Vienna, this is a mere boast on the part of the Turkish Admiral. Possibly, in the far East the news of the conquest of Vienna may have found credence, for the campaigns of Suleiman against Vienna fall about this time.

justice of their request which he granted forthwith; he even went so far as to clothe the Khatib [1] in a robe of honour and to make him ride on an elephant through the city. Ever since that time the name of the Padishah of Turkey has been included in the Bairam prayers, and to whom, I ask, has such honour ever before been vouchsafed?" The Sovereign (Humayun) turning to his nobles said: "Surely the only man worthy to bear the title of Padishah is the ruler of Turkey, he alone and no one else in all the world."

Another time we were talking about the Khan of the Crimea, and I remarked that he also held his office under the Padishah of Turkey. "But," said Humayun, "if that be so how then has he the right of the Khutbe?" "It is a well known fact," I replied, "that my Padishah alone has the power to grant the right of Khutbe and of coinage." This statement seemed to satisfy everybody and we prayed together for the welfare of my Sovereign.

One day the Emperor planned a little excursion on horseback to visit the graves of the holy Sheikhs of Lahore, and I accompanied him. We visited the graves of Shah Kutbeddin the Pir of Delhi, of Sheikh Nizam Weli, Sheikh Ferid Shekr-Ghendj, Mir Khosru

[1] Khatib is the name of the Mollah who on Fridays says the Khutbe or Friday prayer in which the names of the Khalifa and of the local ruler are inserted.

Dehlevi and Mir Husein Dehlevi. When the conversation turned upon the poetical works of Mir Khosru I quoted some of his best poems, and under their influence I conceived a most telling distich. I turned to the Emperor saying, "It would be presumption on my part to measure my powers against those of Mir Khosru [1], but he has inspired me, and I would fain recite my couplet before your Majesty." "Let us hear it," said Humayun, and I recited the following:

"Truly great is only he, who can be content with his daily bread.

For happier is he than all the kings of the earth."

"By God," cried the Monarch, "this is truly sublime!"

It is not so much my object here to make mention of my poetic effusions, but rather to show up Humayun's appreciation of poetry.

On another occasion I called upon Shahin Bey, the keeper of the Imperial Seal, and asked him to use his influence to obtain permission for me to depart. In order not to come empty-handed I brought him two Ghazels, and begged him urgently to intercede

[1] Mir Khosru Dehlevi (i. e. from Delhi) one of the greatest poets of India, born 651 (1253), died, 725 (1324). He wrote in Persian, which language had been introduced into India, with the spread of Islam.

for me. Shahin Bey promised to do his best, and one day he actually brought me the glad news that my petition had been granted, but that I was expected to offer my request formally in verse. The rainy season was now at an end, I wrote to the Monarch, enclosing two Ghazels, which had the desired effect, for I received not only permission to leave, but also presents and letters of safe conduct.

All was ready for the start. Humayun had given audience on Friday evening, when, upon leaving his castle of pleasure, the Muezzin announced the Ezan just as he was descending the staircase. It was his wont, wherever he heard the summons, to bow the knee in holy reverence. He did so now, but unfortunately fell down several steps, and received great injuries to his head and arm. Truly the proverb rightly says, "there is no guarding against fate."

Everything was confusion in the palace, but for two days they kept the matter secret. It was announced to the outer world that the Sovereign was in good health, and alms were distributed amongst the poor. On the third day, however, that was on the Monday, he died of his wounds [1]. Well may the Koran say, "We come from God and to Him do we return."

[1] Elphinstone in the 'History of India' (p. 472), relates his death as follows: "He had been walking on the terrace of his library, and was descending the stairs, (which in such situations

His son Djelaleddin Ekber was at the time away on a journey to visit Shah Ebul Maali, accompanied by the Khanikhanan[1]. He was immediately informed of the sad event. Meanwhile the Khans and Sultans were in the greatest consternation; they did not know how to act. I tried to encourage them and told them how at the death of Sultan Selim the situation was saved by the wisdom of Piri Pasha, who managed to prevent the news of his death from being noised abroad. I suggested that, by taking similar measures, they might keep the Sovereign's death a secret until the Prince should return. This advise was followed. The divan (council of state) met as usual, the nobles were summoned, and a public announcement was made that the Emperor intended to visit his country seat, and would go there on horseback. Soon after, however, it was an-

are narrow steps on the outside of the building and only guarded by an ornamental parapet about a foot high). Hearing the call to prayers from the minarets, he stopped, as is usual on such occasions, repeated the creed and sat down on the steps till the crier had done. He then endeavoured to rise supporting himself on his staff; the staff slipped on the polished marble of the steps and the king fell headlong over the parapet. He was stunned at the time and although he soon recovered his senses, the injury he had received was beyond cure. On the fourth day after his accident he expired in the 49th year of his age and the 26th of his reign, including the 16 years of his banishment from his capital.

[1] This is meant for Bairam Khan, the faithful follower of Humayun and later on the Atabek (tutor) of Ekber.

nounced that on account of the unfavorable weather, the trip had to be abandoned. On the next day a public audience was announced, but as the astrologers did not prophesy favorably for it, this also had to be given up. All this, however, somewhat alarmed the army, and on the Tuesday it was thought advisable to give them a sight of their Monarch. A man called Molla Bi, who bore a striking resemblance to the late Emperor only somewhat slighter of stature, was arrayed in the imperial robes and placed on a throne specially erected for the purpose in the large entrance hall. His face and eyes were veiled. The Chamberlain Khoshhal Bey stood behind, and the first Secretary in front of him, while many officers and dignataries as well as the people from the riverside, on seeing their Sovereign made joyful obeisance to the sound of festive music. The physicians were handsomely rewarded and the recovery of the Monarch was universally credited.

I took leave of all the grandees, and with the news of the Emperor's recovery I reached Lahore about the middle of the month Rebiul Evvel. This was on a Thursday. Travelling by the way of Sani-Pata, Pani-Pata, Kirnat and Tani Sera, I came to Samani [1]

[1] On modern English Maps of India, these names are given as Sonpat, Panipat, Karnal, Tanesar and Samani, in the same order on the way from Delhi to Lahore.

where I communicated the news to the governor that the Padishah (Humayun) was giving audiences, and that he was in good health [1]. From there I went by the road of Sahrandi to Matchuvara [2] and Bachuvara [3] and crossing the Sultanpoor by boat, I returned to Lahore by a forced march. Meanwhile Prince Djelaleddin Ekber had ascended the throne, and in Lahore and many other places, his name was inserted in the Friday prayers. Mirza Shah, the governor of Lahore, however, would not permit me to leave, for he professed to have received orders from the new Emperor that no one was to be allowed to go to Kabul and Kandahar. The only way therefore was to go back to the Emperor (Ekber) and accordingly I went as far as Kelnor where I met Djelaleddin Ekber and the Khanikhanan just opposite the fortress of Mankit [4].

I was informed through Molla Pir Mehemmed [5] the Khodja of Bairam Khan that during the interregnum I should remain where I was, and that in

[1] Very striking is the want of reserve wherewith this lie is spread to serve a political purpose.

[2] Rectius: Matchivara, a town in Penjab in Ludiana.

[3] Perhaps Bachrewan, a town in the province of Oudh?

[4] A stronghold built by Selim Shah on the boundary mountains of Sewalik, against the Sakkars (Elphinstone p. 496).

[5] Elphinstone, 'History of India', page 498, calls this man Pir Mohamed, the teacher or tutor of Ekber, while our author calls him Khodja Bairam Khan.

a short time he would appoint me to some post either in Hind or Sind whichever I preferred. I hastened to produce my ferman given to me by the late Padishah, presenting him at the same time with a chronogramm on the death of his father. My verses pleased the Mirza and after examining the ferman of his father, he gave me leave to continue my journey, stipulating, however, that I should travel in company with the four Begs which he was about to send with troops to Cabul.

Ebul Maali [1], who meanwhile had been taken prisoner, was confined in the castle of Lahore. In return for my chronogramm I received a Lakh for travelling expenses and began to prepare for my journey with the four Begs.

Amongst the many strange and wonderful things I saw in India, I must make mention of a few. The unbelievers are called in Gujarat 'Banian,' and in India 'Hindu.' They do not belong to the Ehli-Kitab [2], and believe in fate (kadem-i-alem). When a man dies his body is burnt by the riverside. If

[1] Ebul Maali, a Said from Kashgar who had entered the service of Humayun in 1551. He had rebelled against Ekber and had taken possession of Kabul, where he was afterwards defeated and imprisoned in Lahore. He died in 1563. (Elphinstone p. 563).

[2] Literally: Believers in the Book; these, therefore, have none of the four Sacred Books, viz. Koran, Tevrat, Gospels and Psalms. Consequently they are Heathen.

the deceased leaves a wife, past childbearing[1] she is not burnt, if, however, she is not past that age she is unconditionally burnt. If a wife of her own free will offers herself to be burnt, the relations celebrate the occasion with great rejoicings. Should the Mahommedans interfere and forcibly prevent the self-sacrifice, fate decrees that their king must die (?), and no other be raised. For this reason, officers of the Padishah are always present on such occasions, to prevent any act of violence[2].

Another curious custom is the use of tame gazelles in hunting. A noose is lightly thrown over their antlers and then they are driven to mix with the wild gazelles. Like seeks like, and the latter soon make up to their tame companions, bringing their heads in close proximity to those of the others. The noose which is round the antlers of the tame animal falls over the head of the other and pulls it down. The more it struggles the more it gets entangled noose, and can not possibly escape. This method is in use all over India.

Buffaloes are very plentiful in the steppes. They

[1] In the text amelden Kalmish عملدن قالمش corresponding to the person عمل مانده amel mande, which is also used to express unfitness for childbearing.

[2] The burning of widows (Suttee) has in recent times been put a stop to by the English, and it is very characteristic that the Moguls had, long before that time, endeavoured to check the custom.

are hunted with elephants. Turrets are placed on the elephant's back in which several men are hidden. Thus they traverse the plain and as soon as the elephant comes up with the buffalo he attacks him with his teeth and holds him till the hunters get off his back and capture him. Wild oxen (Gau-Kutas)[1] are hunted in a similar manner, but they are much stronger than other animals of their kind, and their tongue is supposed to have such force, that they can kill a man with it. The Emperor Humayun once told me a story, to the effect that one of these wild oxen having overtaken a man, flayed him with his tongue from head to foot. The Emperor vouched for the truth of this story with an oath. The best kutas are found in the land of Bahr-itch, perhaps that accounts for their being called Bahri-Kutas (which means sea-kutas), although they belong unquestionably to the terrestrial animals[2]. I might go on enumerating many more interesting and curious things to be seen in India, but it would keep me too long.

About the middle of Rebiul Evvel we left for Kabul. We crossed the River Lahore in ships, and

1 Also called Khutaz and Kudaz, a kind of horned cattle. Their tail is used as an ornament to hang round the horse's neck.

2 Pavet de Courteille: Dictionaire Turk-Oriental, translates قوتاس, by boeuf marin.

came presently to another large stream which had to be crossed. Finding no ships at hand, we built a raft of barrels and chairs [1] and so managed to reach the other side. Next we came to Bahara where another river had to be crossed, this time in ships. When I told the governor (Khodja) of this place what Ekber had commanded, he exclaimed, "God be merciful! As the Padishah was dead we have not collected the taxes, the people still owe them. I will send round, collect the moneys and hand them over to you [2]." Mir Babu's and the other Begs who were of the company, consulted together and decided that as Shah Abul Maali had escaped from his prison in Lahore, and might possible have taken refuge with his brother Kihmerd Bey in Kabul, it would not be safe for them to delay, but they suggested that I should wait till the tribute money was collected, and follow them as soon as I could.

But I argued that the roads were unsafe and dangerous and that it would be much better to keep all together. I acted on the principle, that "The contented mind shall be satisfied and the covetous

[1] In the text. كت ket. i. e. سرير serir, the first being Persian, meaning Barrel, the second Arabian, meaning, throne, chair.

[2] It appears from this passage that the Emperor's guests only received the gifts allotted to them when on their return journey, had in fact to collect them from the authorities of the districts through which they passed.

man shall be humbled." So I relinquished my claim upon the tribute money and continued my journey with the others. After crossing the rivers Khoshab [1] and Nilab [2] in ships, I set foot upon the shore of Bakhtar [3].

XI.

Our experience in Bakhtar-Zemin i. e. in Kabulistan.

In the beginning of the month Djemaziul-Evvel we left the river Nilab and turned towards Kabul. For fear of the Afghans under Adam Khan, we made a quick march through the night, and at daybreak we arrived at the foot of the mountain. So far the Afghans had not seen us, but by the time we had reached the top, there were thousands of them gathered together. We seized our guns, and with God's help managed to get out of their way, and came to the town of Pershuer, i. e. Peshawer. Soon after, we crossed the Khaiber Pass, and reached Djushai. In the mountains we saw two rhinoceroses

[1] Khoshab the name of a town in Penjab, situated on the river Djehlam, and not the name of the river itself, as our author states.

[2] Nilab, blue water, cannot possibly be the river Kabul.

[3] Bakhtar-Zemin = Bakhtarland, i. e. Bactria.

(Kerkedans)[1], each the size of a small elephant; they have a horn on their nose about two inches long. In Abyssinia these animals are much more plentiful.

Presently we reached Laghman[2], and after a very toilsome journey through Hezareland[3], we entered Kabulistan and its capital Kabul. Here I visited the two sons of Humayun, Mehemmed Hekim Mirza, and Ferrukh Fal Mirza; I also saw Mun'im Khan, and, after presenting the ferman from Humayun, I was treated with much honour. Kabul itself is a beautiful city, surrounded by mountains covered with snow, and pleasure gardens with running brooks. Pleasure and merriment prevailed everywhere, feasting and banqueting were the order of the day. In every corner were gaily dressed slender Luli's[4] enticing one with music and song to join the merry crowd; the populace in fact seemed to

[1] کرکدان, generally translated by Rhinoceros. Baber (1356) makes mention of this animal under the name of کرك gherek, and he describes it as being about the size of a buffalo.

[2] Perhaps more correctly Lughman, east of Kabul.

[3] Hezare is the name of the mountainous region, northeast of Peshawer; also the name of an Iranian Mongoltribe, dwelling between Hĕrat and Kabul.

[4] Luli لولی is, in Central Asia, the name given to the Gipsies, to which tribe the dancing and singing damsels and the prostitutes, generally belonged. This used also to be the case in Turkey; comp. Tchenghi = musician, dancing girl, and Tchingane = Gipsy.

have no thought for any thing, but for pleasure and enjoyment.

'Who would long for Huri's and the Paradise whose good fortune has brought him amongst the Luli's of Kabul?'

We, however, had no time for such frivolities, our only aim and object was to reach home as soon as possible. Mun'im Khan remarked that the roads were snowed up, that the Hindu Kush could not possibly be passed, and that it would be far better for us to wait a few days in Kabul; but I quickly replied that men could overcome mountains, if they had the mind to do so. Thereupon the Governor commanded Mir Nezri the Chief of the Ferashi and Peshai, to accompany me, and his men were to conduct our horses and goods safely across the mountainpass. We left accordingly in the beginning of Djemazi ul Evvel and came to Karabag[1] and from there to Tcharikar and Pervane or Mervan.

[1] Kara-bag (black-garden) marked on the maps merely as Bag (garden). Tcharikar lies north of Kabul, and Pervane lies in the same direction as the Pass of that name at the foot of the Hindu Kush. Our author did not take the route now generally used, across the Dendanshiken (tooth-breaker), but the other, which lies more to the east, and which was the one followed by Baber. This is one of the Pervanpasses, which, starting from the place of that same name leads to Badjgah and from there into the valley of Enderab. Comp.: 'A journey to the sources of the river Oxus,' by Capt. John Wood. Published by Yule. LXV.

This was Nezri's native country. He collected his men and they took us across to the other side of the mountain. It was a very difficult passage, but we accomplished it that day and spent the night in a village at the foot of the pass.

XII.

The condition of Badakhshan and Khatlan.

Early in the month of Redjeb we came to the city of Anderab and journeyed from there through Badakhshan to Talikan where I had an interview with Suleiman Shah [1] and his son Ibrahim Mirza. On the day of our arrival the Mirza had met us, and received me in his pleasure garden; I offered him some presents and a Ghazel. The Mirza, who understood poetry, entered into a poetical competition with me, and introduced me next day to his father to whom I also offered gifts and a Ghazel. The Sovereign also showed me much attention and loaded me with signs of his favour. There was hostility between Pir Mohammed Khan the ruler of Balkh

[1] Suleiman Shah was the son of Khan Mirza the Wise, a cousin of Baber's. He had usurped the throne of Bedakhshan in 1508, and was afterwards established by Humayun as ruler over the whole of the Upper-Oxus-territory.

and Borak Khan the ruler of Transoxania, and the roads were made unsafe, the more so as Pir Mohammed's younger brother had raised a revolt in Kunduz, Kavadian, and Termed, which districts were now in great tumult. They advised me therefore to travel by the way of Badakhshan and Khatlan [1], and both Suleiman and his son presented me with horses and garments of honour, besides giving me a letter of recommendation to Djihanghir Ali the ruler of Khatlan who had married his younger sister; and so I journeyed to Kishm the capital of Badakhshan [2]. I saw the Sovereign's pleasure garden, and Humayun's garden Duabe, and proceeded from Kalai Zafar [3] to Rustak and from there to Bender Semti [4]. I approached Dalli in Khatlan from the Kashgar (eastern?) side, and made a pilgrimage to the grave of Seid Ali Hamadani, and from there I went to Kulaba [5] where

[1] From the political condition already referred to, it is quite evident why our author chose this very difficult, roundabout route past Badakhshan, the same route which was taken by Sheibani Khan, Baber's adversary, during his campaign against Khosru Shah. Part of ancient Khatlan, also called Khotl, is now included in the Province of Kulab.

[2] Feizabad is now the capital of Badakhshan. It was Suleiman Shah who made Kishm his residence.

[3] Kalai Zafar (castle of victory), is situated on the Koktche a tributary of the Oxus.

[4] Now Semti, on the left side of the Pendje.

[5] Now Kulab, (1810 ft. above the sea), situated on a tributary of the Oxus.

I met with Djihanghir Ali Khan, and after presenting my letter of recommendation, he gave me an escort of 50 men to conduct me to Charsui where I crossed the Pul-i-Senghin [1] (stone bridge), and dismissed the men who had escorted us.

XIII.

Events in Turan, i. e. Transoxania.

On the day that I crossed the bridge, I first set foot on Transoxanian soil. After a day's rest I proceeded to Bazar No (New-Market), and from there to a little place called Tchiharshembe, where I visited the grave of the Khodja Yaakub Tcharkhi. Then on to Tchaganian, i. e. Hissar-i-Shadman [2]. I visited Timur Sultan, the Kagalga [3] (قاغالغه) of the Ozbeg rulers and passed mount Senghirdek [4] where it always

[1] Neither Charsui nor Pul-i-Senghin are to be found on any modern map, but as the author identifies Hissar with Chaganian, i. e. places the former in the dominion of the latter province, we may take it, that the Kafirnihan-river was then the boundary line of Transoxania.

[2] Hissar, situated at the confluence of the Ilek and the Khanka-Derya, formerly known as Hissar-i-Shadman.

[3] Probably an ancient title which in its present form is not mentioned in any lexicons or vocabularies.

[4] Senghirdek is mentioned on the modern maps of Central-Asia, between Sehri-Sebz and Sari-Asiya (Yellow Mill), as the name of a stream and of a place, but not as the name of a mountain. Seng-ghirdek means: a stone tent.

rains and a considerable stream is formed at the foot of the mountain, and I marvelled at the wonderful works of God. The next station was Sehri-Sebz, i. e. Kesh, where I met Hashim Sultan who gave me permission to continue my journey to Samarkand. With great difficulty we got across the mountain [1] situated between the two last named places; we touched the little town of Mazar and in the beginning of Shaaban we reached Samarkand, which is a perfect paradise. Here I saw Borak Khan [2] (more correctly called Noruz Ahmed), who, in return for my humble offerings, gave me a horse and garments of honour. It was this same Borak Khan to whom his Majesty the Padishah had sent cannon and guns by the hand of Sheikh's Abdullātif and Dadash. At the time of my arrival Abdullātif Khan, the ruler of Samarkand, was dead [3], and Borak had taken his place. Pir Mohammed Khan in Balkh, and Burhan Seid Khan [4]

[1] This must be mount Karatepe (Black Hill) (5181 ft).

[2] Borak Khan, a son of Mahmud Khan, who was defeated by Sheibani. He was a native of the steppes in the Northeast of Transoxania, and, favoured by the bad government of Burhan Khan he and his horsemen, consisting of Kirghises and Kalmuks, invaded the land, and took possession of the capital, Samarkand. He died in the year 963 (1555). The incidents connected with his reign, which our author mentions, are the more valuable to us as we find no mention of them anywhere else.

[3] He died in the year 959 (1551).

[4] Called by abbreviation Burhan Khan, an uncle of Obeidullah. He reigned only a short time and died in 964 (1556).

in Bokhara, declared their independence, and Borak's first business was to settle this matter. He began by taking Samarkand and proceeded to Shehri Sebz, where a great battle was fought, in which the Ketkhuda (overseer) of the Osman soldiers fell. He then took the stronghold and marched to Bokhara, which place he laid siege to. Seid Burhan, the ruler of Bokhara, made peace with Borak, relinquished the place to him, and retired to Karakul where the brother of Pir Mohammed Khan then reigned. He, however, gave up the place to Seid Burhan. When Borak Khan entered Samarkand, the Aga of the Osmans [1] had just started with a few men on their way to Turkey, having taken the way of Tashkend and Turkestan. Ahmed Tchaush was also on the point of returning to Turkey by the way of Bokhara and Kharezm, for part of the Janissaries had enlisted under Seid Burhan and the remainder joined his son. About 150 remained faithful to Borak Khan. When he had communicated all this to me he added: "I am now as a liar before his Majesty the Sultan of Turkey, for I can do nothing, but if thou wilt

[1] Aga of the Osmans, was the title of a commander of the Janissaries which Sultan Suleiman had sent from Constantinople to Samarkand to support the authority of the Eastern Turks. Our author therefore came here unexpectedly in contact with his countrymen.

help me, something may yet be done." He offered me the government of a Province, but I said that with such a small army nothing could be done, moreover that, without the consent of my Padishah, I could not stir in the matter. He thereupon proposed to send an envoy to the Sublime Porte to explain the situation. As a matter of fact he had already decided to send Sadr Alem, a descendant of Khodja Ahmed Jesewi [1], and gave him a letter, in which he expressed his willingness in the future to satisfy every wish of the Sultan. He discharged me however. During my stay in Samarkand I made a pilgrimage to the grave of the prophet Daniel, to the place of the Khidr (Elias), to the cloak and to the wooden shoes of the prophet, and also to the Koran, written by Ali himself [2]. Besides these places I visited the graves of the following sheikhs and sages: the author of Hidayet, Ebu Mansur Matridi; Shah-Zinde, Khodja

[1] Khodja Ahmad Jesewi, the Patronsaint of Turkestan, whose grave in Aulia Ata is to this day eagerly visited by pilgrims. See my, "Geschichte Buchara's," II. pp. 38 and 205. See also my "Tchagataische Sprachstudien," p. 115.

[2] When in Samarkand I could learn nothing about the cloak and the Naalin (wooden shoes) of tbe Prophet, but the copy of the Koran here referred to, was extant in the Mausoleum of Timur. This latter however although a very old Manuscript in Kufi letters, has not descended from Kaliph Ali, nor yet from Kaliph Osman; it has been brought to Turkestan by the descendants of Khodja Ahrar, and from Samarkand the Russians took it to St. Petersburg.

Abdullah, Khodja Abdi-birun, Khodja Abdi-derum, the Tchopanata, and the Kazizade of Rum, and the grave of the 444.000 Transoxanian sages.

But to return to Borak Khan. One day, while talking together, he asked me which of all the cities I had visited pleased me most. I replied with the following stanza:

'Far from home no one longs for Paradise.
For in his eyes his native town is superior even [to Bagdad.'

"Thou hast spoken well," said the Khan.

Now as regards the embassage to Constantinople Sadr Alem proposed to go by Turkestan, but when he was told that the Nogai tribe of the Mangit committed violence upon travellers and that the roads swarmed with robbers and highwaymen, who gave no quarter to musulmans[1], but plundered and ill-treated any that came in their way, he decided to travel through Bokhara.

Unfortunately, just then the news came that Seid Burhan had again declared war with Borak Khan, and that the latter's son Kharezm Shah had been attacked. Borak Khan advised me thereupon to

[1] Consequently they belonged at that time still to the Shaman faith, an interesting fact and easily explained when we consider that at the time of Timur, both Kirghizes and Turkomans are described as heathen.

remain at Ghidjduvan until the return of the envoy. If no hostilities took place we might travel by that way, but otherwise we were to wait until he sent someone to conduct us safely through Bokhara. To this I agreed. On the fifth of Ramazan we started, touched Kala and Kermineh, crossed the river of Samarkand[1] at Duabe, and so arrived at Ghidjduvan[2], where I visited the grave of Khodja Abdul Khalik.

As the Mirza (?) was not here, and no news concerning him could be obtained, we went on to Pul Rabat. Meanwhile the troops of Prince Kharezm Shah had prepared for battle[3]. Suddenly Khan Ali Bey, the Prince's tutor, accosted us with the question whither we were going. When I replied: "to Bokhara," he said: "Seid Burhan the ruler of Bokhara threatens to attack Prince Kharezm Shah, and we pray thee to help us." "How now!" I cried, "we help no man; Borak Khan has not requested us to do so; on the contrary, he has charged us to go to Ghidjduvan,

1 Its name is Zerefshan or Kohik.

2 Ghidjduvan the most northerly town of the Khanate on the Wafkend river.

3 In the text كايم و كاجيم keyim re kedjim, more correctly, kiyim ve kedjim = full equipment, the first word (kiyim) meaning armour of the warrior, the second (kedjim), equipment of the horses, from kidje, felt, because the trappings of the horses were made of hard felt. Comp. كيكيم with Pavet de Courbeille. Dictionnaire Turk-Oriental, p. 483.

and there to await the return of the envoy. So we continued on our way. As we approached Minar (Spire) about 100 redcoats (Ala tehapan)[1] rushed down upon us crying: "In the name of the Mirza turn back," and at the same time they struck one of my companions. Immediately we prepared to fight, when a Seid sprang forward and commanded the Ozbegs to stop. Both sides held back and the Seid announced that the Mirza sent us greeting and desired us not to proceed any further but to look on from a distance. So we were compelled to turn back. With ten of my companions I had an interview with the Mirza who renewed his request that we should help him; but I refused again, whereupon ten guns were forcibly taken from us and we were commanded to remain mere spectators. The Prince's bearing was very haughty before he had sighted the enemy, for as the proverb says:

'Our own fist is always of iron,
Until we receive the first box on the ear.'

But no sooner had Seid Burhan appeared in sight, from the opposite direction, then the Prince retreated across the bridge to the Rabat (Karvanserai). I went on with six companions, which I left behind me in the court of the kiosk. Seid Burhan advanced with 1000

[1] May stand for coloured coat, and merely indicates the distinguishing colour of the regiment.

Kizil-Ayaks [1], i. e. young men from Bokhara, and 40 Turkish archers, therefore well equipped for war. In a moment he defeated the Prince, who, being wounded by a bullet, took flight, leaving his colours, musical and other military instruments behind him on the battlefield. Of my three companions which fled with the Prince, one was wounded by a lance and died soon after, and while the others retreated with the Ozbegs into the Rabat where they were attacked by Seid Burhan, I went on to meet the army to enquire after the Mirza, leaving my horse in charge of two men. I heard that he was quartered close to the Rabat, and asked to be conducted into his presence, and just as I was crossing the bridge, attended by a few men, some villain wounded me with an arrow. This was the signal for a general attack, swords were raised on all sides and I was very near losing my life.

Fortunately the attack had been witnessed by the Osmans serving under the Khan; they had recognised me and came to my rescue, calling out: "This man is the guest of our Prince, what then is the meaning of this?" The Ozbeghi (commander of 10 men), immediately stopped the attack and apprized the Khan of what had taken place, whereupon the

[1] Literally, Red-feet, meaning people that go bare-footed, hence the expression, vagabond, and vagrant.

latter, a glorious youth, hastened to me, embraced me, and begged my forgiveness, for it was by accident, he said, that I had become mixed up in the battle and I had been attacked on the principle of the proverb which says: 'Wet and dry burns together.' He commissioned two officers to conduct us over the bridge, during which transport two more of my people were attacked and received swordwounds. I lost on this occasion a beautiful led-horse, all my cooking apparatus, one pack-horse and 10 saddle-horses which were stolen by the soldiers. With much difficulty I got across the bridge and while I was resting at a little distance, the Khan, to please me, ordered the Turkish soldiers stationed in the Rabat to hand the place over to me, as we were innocent and free from all reproach. As I approached the place I called out: "Stop fighting, I am here and the Khan will pardon you for my sake." Thus the Rabat fell into my hands and with it some of the lost horses, but many of the firearms were irrevocably lost. My two men, who had been taken prisoner in the fight, had escaped, and so we proceeded to the town which we reached that night. Seid Burhan spoke thus to me: "Be thou my guide in this and in the next world; this land shall henceforth belong to thy Padishah, thou shalt rule in Bokhara and I will retire to Karakol." "Not so," was my reply, "if thou gavedst me the whole land of Transoxania I could not stay here. Know, oh Khan! that I shall report before the Sublime Porte, the injustice which has been done to thee, and my glorious Padishah will be gracious unto thee, and possibly the government of these provinces will be entrusted to thy care." These words pleased the Khan, he gave a banquet in my honour and showed me much kindness, and during the fortnight which I spent in Bokhara he visited me every day in the pleasure garden which served as my residence. I composed a Ghazel in his honour which highly delighted him and led to many poetical discussions. When at last I desired permission to continue my journey, he demanded of me that I should give him our iron guns in exchange for his brass ones. He pressed me so hard that I was compelled to give in, and received 40 brass muskets in return for all the iron ones which we had left. I also had to exchange my led-horse for a gelding, besides giving him two precious books.

Meanwhile the envoy from Borak Khan had arrived, who apologized to me for his son (Kharezm Shah), and made peace with Seid Burhan through the mediation of the Ghidjduvani Abdul Sultan. Thus peace and security were once more restored.

I delayed in Bokhara to make pilgrimages to the

graves of Bahaeddin Nakishbendi, Kazi Khan, Tchar Bekir, Khodja Ebn Hifz Kebir, Sadr esh Sheriat, Tadj esh Sheriat, Seid Mir Kelal (the spiritual head of Baha-eddin,) Sultan Ismail the Samanide, Eyub and Sarakhsi, and after that I journeyed to Kharezm.

Our way led first to Karakol, then to Farab where we crossed the Oxus in ships, and early in the month Shavvāl I touched Iranian soil, namely Khorasan. The first town I stopped at was Tchardjui [1], where I visited the grave of Khodja Meshed, a brother of Imam Ali Musa [2]. Then we took the road through the wilderness [3] to Kharezm. By day and by night we had to wage war against lions [4], it was not safe for one man to go alone to draw water; but at last, after 10 days of unutterable weariness, we reached Hezaresp [5] and from there in five days, Khiva [6], where I visited the grave of Pehlevan Mahmud Pir.

[1] Tchardjui (more correctly Tchihar-djui = four brooks, after four tributairies of the Oxus which are there), was at that time Persian territory, and came only to be reckoned to Bokhara after the seizure of Abdullah Khan.

[2] Name of the shiite Saint in Meshed.

[3] Consequently the left side of the river.

[4] Curious it seems that 300 years ago, lions were so plentiful in those parts, while in modern times there has been no sign of them in the steppes of Turkestan.

[5] In the text called Hezarus, by mistake.

[6] It appears strange that our author consistently writes Khiva, whereas Abulghazi who wrote 100 years later uses خیوق Khiwak the older form of the word.

XIV.

Our experiences in Kharezm and Deshti-Kipchak.

Towards the end of Shavval we left Khiva and in five days we came to Kharezm where I made the acquaintance of Dost Mohammed Khan and his brother Esh-Sultan [1]. I visited the graves of Sheikh Nedjmeddin Kubera, Sheikh Ali Rametin, Sheikh Khalweti Yan, Imam Mohammed Bari'i, Sahib Kuduri, Djar Ullah Ulama, Molla Husein Kharezmi (the expounder of the Koran), Seid Ata, and Hekim Ata.

When it was brought to my knowledge that the holy Sheikh Abdullatif had died in the city of Vezir, I could not rest until I had made a pilgrimage to his grave in company with a few friends. As this saint had been moreover my spiritual adviser in Sufism, I recited the whole Koran over his grave, to insure for him everlasting peace and bliss in Paradise. We also cooked a pilaf, (a rice dish) and I prepared a Chronogramm in commemoration of his death.

[1] Dost Mohammed Khan, or simply Dost, who was then the ruler of Kharezm, and his brother Esh-Sultan, were both sons of Budjuga Khan. Their rival to the throne was Hadjim Khan, who conquered both in turn and put them to death. (Comp. Abulghazi: Edition Desmaison, p. 236).

Having received letters of commendation to the Manghit chiefs, from Hadji Mohammed Sultan, Timur Sultan and Mahmud Sultan, the three sons of Agatai Khan, I returned to Kharezm where Sheikh Sadr Alem, the envoy of Borak Khan had meanwhlle also arrived. Our party consisted besides ourselves of the wife of Sheikh Husein of Kharezm (daughter of Makhdum Aazam), the Sheikh's son, and a few moslems; we travelled in carriages. Most of the company wore clothes of sheepskin and they wanted us to do the same, for they said, the Manghit[1] are worse even than the Ozbegs and when they see strangers they invariably take them for Russians[2], which is synonimous to saying, they attack them. Thus we were compelled to don the outlandish garb (sheepskin), for, as I said to encourage my people: 'A wise man follows the ways of the world and makes no trouble of it.'

Thus equipped we started in the first days of Zilkaada. For more than a month we wandered about in the Deshti Kipchak (Kirghiz steppe). It

[1] The tribe of the Manghit, now belonging to the settled population of Khiwa, seems at that time still to have led a nomadic life, inhabiting the steppe between the Aral and the Caspian sea, now the home of the Kirghizes.

[2] The Nomads of Central Asia feared the Russians, for three years before that time (1554), Czar Ivan Wassilyewich had conquered Astrakhan.

was late in the autumn, and at that time of the year not a bird, not a wild ass (Onagre) can be seen, for there is not a vestige of verdure, not a drop of water to be found. It was one interminable wilderness; one desert steppe. At last we came to a place called Sham and shortly after to Saraidjik [1] where we met some Hadji's and three of the Moslems which had been discharged at Samarkand. These latter were quite naked, and at sight of us they cried: "Whither go ye? Astrakhan is taken by the Russians, Ahmed Tchaush has fought a battle with them and our Aga has been plundered by the troops of Arslan Mirza. The way is blocked, be warned and go back." In vain I quoted the lines:

"We are but poor beggars, what harm can [befall us?
For ten armed men cannot rob one who [has nothing."

The rest of the company, especially the merchants, were not of my opinion; they proposed to

[3] (see page 80). By Deshti-Kipchak = the steppe of the Kipchaks, oriental writers understand the steppe situated between Kharezm and the Volga territory. Ibn Batuta likewise accomplished the distance between Kharezm (now Urghendj) and Saraidjik in 30 days.

[1] Saraidjik, small palace on the bank of the Ural, about one hour's distance from the Caspian Sea. Jenkinson in 1558 found the place still intact, but Pallas in the past century found only extensive ruins to indicate the place.

delay a few days in Kharezm and await events for:

"Speed is from the Devil and patience is from God."

The envoy and the other Moslems were of the same mind, and so I reluctantly retraced my steps to Kharezm. The envoy returned to Samarkand, but all the rest remained in Kharezm, and when Dost Mohammed Khan, the ruler of Khiva, enquired of me by which route I now proposed to travel, I replied, "I will go by the way of Meshhed in Khorasan to Irak Adjemi and from there to Bagdad." Thereupon the Khan said: "Remain here with us. In the Spring the Manghits seek their pastures, possibly the Russians may also quit the land by that time, and, remember, the way to Bagdad is long."

But I could not agree to this and in support of my argument I quoted the proverb: 'To the lover Bagdad is not far distant[1];' so at last the Khan had to give in. He agreed to my departure, gave me a beautiful horse, and to my companions he gave the carriage in which we had travelled up to here. As regards our route my first plan was to travel by the way of the Caspian sea and Shirvan, but my companions did not like this, because the musulman army which had lately broken up from Kaffa[2] had become involved in a bloody war with Abdullah Khan,

[1] 'Ashika Bagdad irak deyildir,' a well-known Turkish proverb.

[2] Ancient Theodosia in the Crimea.

who would not permit any Turks to pass that way. Next we made enquiries about the roads of Circassia, past Demir-Kapu, but we heard that the Circassians had raised a revolt. There remained therefore only the way of Khorasan and Irak, and concerning these districts we learned that the Persian King was in perfect harmony with our glorious Padishah [1], but that the Bey of Kizilbash (the Shiite officer) would probably prevent us from obtaining admittance to the Shah. I thought to myself, 'Where God does not slay, man's attempts are but futile;' moreover, 'they who fear death, should not venture on travels;' — so after duly consulting the horoscope [2], and having made quite sure that there was no other way open to us, I decided to travel through Persia. The camels were hired and all was ready; I went to take leave of Dost Mohammed, the ruler of Khiva who remarked casually that it was quite impossible for us to travel with firearms through the enemy's land. Thereupon

[1] At that time the King of Persia was Thamasp Shah, and it so happened that he was on friendly terms with Sultan Suleiman, for about this time a gorgeous ambassy was sent by the ruler of the Ottoman empire to Kazvin, as recorded by Rauzat es Sefa in the VIIIth Book.

[2] Istikhare = Horoscope, is consulted by opening the Koran at hazard and the passage at which it opens gives the answer. Another way is by the throwing of dice, or by seizing the rosary (Tesbih) at hasard, when the even or uneven number of the beads decides the question.

we gave half of our arms to the Khan, and the other half to his younger brother Esh Sultan. We received a letter of commendation to Ali Sultan a brother of Tin Sultan, and being well stocked with provisions and large skins for water, and trusting in God, we started on our journey to Kharezm in the beginning of the month Zilhidje.

XV.

Our Fate in Khorasan.

By divine grace we got safely across the Oxus[1] and encamped on the opposite shore, awaiting the arrival of the rest of our party. While there, the wife of Sheikh Husein sent me a message to say that she had had a dream in which she had seen her father, the holy Makhdum Aazam, who had come

[1] This passage is of special geographical interest. As our author came from Kharezm on the left shore of the Oxus and crossed the river on his way to Khorasan he refers here undoubtedly to the old course of this river, mentioned by Abulgazi. As the Oxus in its course downstream from Tchardjui, reveals several old riverbeds, the direction here indicated by Sidi Ali must be one of the two courses which ran either from Hezaresp or from Khanka in south-westerly direction into the Caspian Sea. Most likely it was the latter branch, as it was at that time the more important of the two, and according to Abulgazi, culture had reached a considerable height along its shores.

from Vezir to Kharezm in company with another holy sage. Arrived in the town he had thus addressed the people, who welcomed him joyfully: "Mir Sidi Ali has read the Koran over my grave in Vezir, and he has supplicated for my patronage. I have therefore come to help him and to lead him safely through Khorasan." This message filled me with joy. I struck camp next morning and the day following we arrived in Dorum [1]; we passed through, unmolested by Mahmud Sultan and proceeded to Bagwai [2], which place we also passed, without being hindered by Pulad Sultan, and came to Nesa [3]. Here I found Ali Sultan, former governor of Merw, and brother of Tin Sultan, to whom I offered my letter of commendation from Esh Sultan, and was allowed free passage, for every body in these parts is devoted to his Majesty our Padishah. Thus we came to Bawerd (Abiwerd) [4] and Tus where I visited the graves of Imam Mohammed Hanifi and of the poet Firdusi; and on the first of Muharram of the year 964, I reached Meshhed-i-

1 This is Derum, frequently mentioned by Abulgazi, as situated on the old road from Kharezm to Khorasan.

2 Bagwai, on the same road, but is now no longer marked on the map.

3 Nesa, frequently mentioned in the middle ages, situated in the North of Persia. Its ruins have been visited by many modern travellers in the neighbourhood of Ashkabad.

4 Abiwerd is more correct; it is the modern Kahka, a station on the Trans-Caspian-line.

Khorasan, where I immediately made a pilgrimage to the grave of Imam Ali Musa Riza, the prince of Khorasan.

When at sea, during the great storm some time ago, I had vowed to give a Tumen to the Imam; now I fulfilled my vow, and paid a Tumen to Mutawali (the overseer of the Mosque and Mausoleum) and I also paid a Tumen to the Seid. In Meshhed I found Ibrahim Mirza the son of Behram Mirza, who occupied the throne there; also Suleiman Mirza the son of the Shah, and his Vekil (representative) called Kökche Khalipha, who entertained me at a banquet.

In the course of our conversation, these gentlemen naturally wished to draw me into an argument upon the succession and sanctity of the Khaliphs Ali, Ebubekr, Omar and Osman; but I acted upon the principle that silence is the best answer to give a fool, and I was silent. They pressed me, however, and I told them the story of Khodja Nasreddin who was once asked to read the Koran in the Mosque, to which he had replied, 'this is not the place.' "And now," I said, "I have not come hither to argue with you, and I refuse to be questioned." It was with great difficulty that I at last rid myself of them [1].

[1] Curious enough the same custom still prevails in Persia, for when I visited this land three hundred years later, disguised as an Osmanli, I had much to suffer from the indiscretion of the

One of the guests, unfortunately, was a miscreant, of the name of Ghazi Bey; he gave vent to his wrath in these words: "It is not seemly to send such people as these to the Shah. How do we know that they may not kill the men that we give them as an escort, and then take flight. Very possibly they belong to the Ottomans that were sent to Borak Khan, or perhaps they are the bearers of a secret correspondence, and it might be advisable to search them."

The Mirza (Ibrahim) approved of this plan, and the next morning 200 men in armour (kurdji) surrounded the kervanserai and took us prisoners. As the proverb says: "Those who can not be caught by fair means, will be by foul play."

We were each of us put in charge of one of the guards; I was taken to the apartment of the Kökche Khalipha, with my two attendants. My horses were given in another man's charge, and my other effects were entrusted to Mutawali's keeping. They made us undress, and as it was winter we suffered much from the cold. The next day the Mirza took from me all my official papers and sundry letters which I had received from different princes, and had them all put into a bag and sealed.

Shiite fanatics. By night and by day, on the march and at rest, it was always this same vexed question of the succession, which had to be discussed.

When my companions saw this they trembled for their lives, but I comforted them with the sayings "He who falls through no mistake of his, will not shed tears," and "Since fate has not forgotten to bring thee in to this world, it will not forget to take thee out of it," and further "Patience is the key to the final goal."

So we calmly resigned ourselves to our fate. A little later on all were put in chains, except myself; but I was strictly guarded by five men. This action of the Mirza troubled me not a little, and although I tried to make light of it, my heart was very heavy. I wrote a Ghazel to comfort myself, and with the inspiring thoughts suggested by it fresh in my mind, I fell asleep, and being in a semi-conscious state, a divine inspiration in the form of a Murabba [1] was vouchsafed to me, which I sent to Mutawali. This composition caused great excitement among the nobility of the place. About the same time one of the attendants of the Imam declared (whether it was true or feigned I cannot say) that in his dream he had seen the Khaliph Ali, who had charged him to go and set Mir Sidi Ali free. The news of this dream spread rapidly through the town and stirred up the people, whose sympathies were now all turned in my favour.

[1] Murabba = Quatrain, a poem consisting of four lined verses.

Mutawali and Seid went to the Mirza and said: "This man came on a pilgrimage to visit the shrine of the Imam. He is under a vow and desires to go to the Shah. As the Shah is on friendly terms with the Padishah of Turkey it is not right that we should in any way trouble this pilgrim now in the Ashura [1] days. If the man be a traitor, it is sure to come to light, for as the Koran says, 'A traitor is known by his countenance,' and there need be no further question of suspicion." These words of the wise man and of Seid did not lose their effect upon the Mirza. From my side I pointed ont to him the unreliableness of the information upon which he had acted, and in order further to enlist his sympathies in my favour I sent him three poems, after which, partly for fear of the Shah, and partly regretting his rash deed, he gave us our liberty on the 10th of Ashura. He loaded me with presents and gave another banquet in my honour. He also restored to us our horses and our clothes; but many of my other possessions I never recovered. Four valuable books were taken and the whole of my correspondence was conveyed by his armourbearer [2] Ali Bey

1 Ashura days, the first 10 days of the Month Muharram, which, especially in the Shiite part of Persia, were kept as holy days.

2 In the text قپچاجی باشی kapchadji-bashi, may mean chief keeper of the purse from kapcha = purse, or chief armourbearer from kopcha = armour.

and a Yassaul to the Shah in a sealed bag, the transport being effected on a barrow about the middle of Muharram of the said year. Travelling in the same Caravan with us was one of the wives of the Shah and one of the wives of Behram Mirza, who were both returning from a pilgrimage to the shrine of the Imam. I made their acquaintance and they treated us kindly. By my advise my companions comported themselves with due courtesy and modesty towards the retinue of these ladies, mindful of the saying: "The peace of two worlds depends on two things only, courtesy to friends and flattery to foes."

Arrived in Nishabur I visited the graves of Imamzade Mohammed Mahruk, and of Sheikh Attar (ferideddin). Here I also met with Aga Kemal, the Vekil of Khorasan, who, however, did not interfere with us. In Sebzevar we met with a little hostility, but acting on the principle that 'barking dogs bite not,' we soon got free from these firebrands and continued on our way.

XVI.

Our Vicissitudes in Irak-Adjem.

Arrived in the Province of Irak we skirted the

Demavend range, travelling from Mazendran to Bestam, where we visited the graves of Mohammed Aftah, Sheikh Bayazid Bestami, and Sheikh Ebulhasan Harkani. The next day we reached Damgan.

That night one of our company called Ramazan the pious, and known as Bölük Bashi [1], had a dream. Bayazid Bestami with 40 Dervishes had appeared unto him and had spoken thus: "Let us pray for the safe return of Mir Sidi Ali." The Sheikh moreover had written a passport and sealed it, "that we might not be molested by the way." — This was his dream and when I heard of it I rejoiced greatly and thanked God for his mercy vouchsafed; for this message (from the dead), virtually saved my life. After visiting the grave of Imam Djafar in Damgan, we proceeded to Semnan, where we visited the grave of Sheikh Ala-ed-Dowleh Semnani. In this place they tried to draw us into sectarian controversies, but I restrained my comrades, and reminded them of the Hadis, which says: "Ustur zahbak, zahabek in mazhabak," i. e. hide thy gold, thine opinions and thy faith; and I argued with them saying, "Not one of you has travelled more then I have, and experience has made me wise. A wise man does not heed the words of the vulgar and the ignorant."

[1] Bölük-Bashi a degree of rank amongst the Janissaries, literally: captain of a division.

They saw the wisdom of my words, and acted upon my advise.

Before long we came to Rei [1] where I made pilgrimages to the graves of Imam Abdul Azim, and of Bibi Shehrbanu the consort of Imam Husein. Here I also met Mohammed Khudabend a son of the Shah's, and the Kurdji-bashi [2] Sevindek Aga. Their presence was accounted for in this way: Some time ago the Shah had sent Ismail Mirza from Kazvin to Herat, and had now recalled him to Kazvin. The reason of this was that certain things which had happened during his rule had come to light, and by command of the Shah one of the nobles of Kazvin had been executed, and in like manner, also by order of the Shah, some followers of Ismail had been put to death. After this the Shah commanded Prince Mohammed Khudabend to appear before him and the Kurdji-bashi was sent to fetch him. I was very pleased to meet the Prince who assured me of the unwavering devotion of the Shah to our glorious Padishah.

Journeying from Rei it took us a month and a half (to the end of Safar) before we reached Kazvin, the capital of Irak [3].

[1] In the immediate vicinity of Teheran.

[2] Kurdji-bashi = chief armourbearer.

[3] This surely must mean a month and a half after entering Persia,

Upon the Shah being told of our arrival we were none of us allowed to enter the city, but had to take up our quarters in Sebzeghiran, one of the neighbouring villages, under the protection of Mohammed Bey, the Divan Bey [1] of the Great Vizier Maasum Bey. Presently the Ishik Agasi [2] arrived, who took down our names, and the number of our horses, and gave his people private instructions to watch us strictly at night, until further orders.

We were told that the Shah was very angry that we had been allowed to leave Meshhed without any further enquiry, and that in consequence of this Kökche Khalipha and Mir Munshi (first secretary) had been deprived of office. Following up this information, the Kapchadji [3], Ali Bey, came to us by order of Yassaul Pir Ali, and said: "The people here have evil intentions, if you have any ready money about you, give it to me to keep, and if Providence deliver you out of this plight, I will return it; if on the other hand evil should befall you it is better that your riches should fall in the hands of friends than of foes."

for the distance from Rei (Teheran) to Kazvin can easily be accomplished in two or three days. Kazvin was at that time the capital of Persia.

[1] Divan Bey = first secretary.

[2] Ishik Agasi = chief porter, a sort of master of the ceremonies.

[3] See note on page 89.

But I replied: "People who have wandered so long in foreign parts carry no cash about them, and they who fear death do not venture so far from home. I believe in the words of the Koran: 'He who is appointed to die, cannot delay the hour, and without God's permission no man can slay.'"

It so happened that the Shah had by this time examined the letters which had been conveyed to him in a sealed bag, and the ladies who had travelled with us, bore witness that we were poor and harmles folk. Moreover I had sent the Shah a Quatrain which had found much favour, so he set us free. The Shah commanded his Vekil[1], Maasum Bey, to offer me a banquet, after which he would himself entertain me. Maasum Bey was also commissioned to give me the glad news, that I was free to go where I liked, and as an envoy was shortly to be sent to the Sublime Porte, I might, if I liked, travel by the way of Azerbaidjan i. e. by Tebriz and Van. Thereupon I requested that my desire might be made known to the Shah. I said, "we are not prepared to meet the hardships of the Van road in the wintertime, and we beg to be allowed to travel by the way of Bagdad;" which request he graciously granted.

Literally: Representative; at the court of the Shah it is also the title of the overseer over the culinary department.

On the second day we were invited by the Sha to a banquet, and I presented my humble offerings. During the feast we conversed upon poetical and other subjects and the Shah remarked to his courtiers: "These men do not look like intriguers, they are only pilgrims and religious fanatics," — and on the strength of this verdict Kökche Khalipha and Mir Munshi were re-instated in their office. I received a horse and two changes of robes, a bale of silk and several other things; the two Serdars received each two robes of honour, and my five travelling companions, each one. Altogether the Shah behaved handsomely to us and showed a marked respect for the person of his Majesty the Padishah.

One day I was invited to a banquet in the large Music hall, all the Beys of the royal family being present. To give some idea of the magnificence here displayed I will only mention that from five hundred to one thousand Tumens[1] had been spent on the decoration of the hall. There were some hundreds of velvet and silken brocaded carpets, painted and embroidered in figurative designs; quantities of

[1] In the text تومنه اولمش در tumene olmush dur — is not quite clear. Tumen means ducat in Persian, but as the word is here used in the dative, it would appear that something has been omitted.

rious cushions and exquisitely artistic tents, nopies, and sunshades.

Yüzbashi Hasan Bey, one of the Shah's confidents turned to me and said: "Is not this indeed a treasure house?" "It is," I replied, "yet the wealth of kings is not measured by their gold and silver but by their military power." This remark silenced him; he did not return to the subject.

As the envoy had already started for Tebriz I was detained for another month, during which time the Shah showed me much attention and I spent a good deal of my time in his presence. One day he ventured the remark: "Why were those 300 Janissaries sent from Turkey to assist Borak Khan?" I answered that these had not been sent to strenghten Borak Khan's forces, but merely as an escort to the late Sheikh Abdullatif, because it was a well known fact that the Circassians [1] had killed Baba Sheikh, a son of the holy Ahmed Jesewi on the road from Astrakhan, and that that route was there-

[1] The Circassians were at that time not yet Mohammedans, for they were converted later on by Ferrukh Pasha.

It appears from this passage that the Pilgrimsroute from Central Asia to Mecca led in those days past Astrakhan, i. e. by Kharezm and the lower Volga, and from there across the Caucasus via Constantinople to Arabia, about the same as in modern times, when pilgrims travel by the Transcaspian line, via Batum Baku and Constantinople to Mecca.

To this he could make no reply and I turned the conversation into another channel.

The Shah once said to me, "Tell me, since thou hast travelled so much, which of the cities thou hast visited, pleases thee best." And I replied: "I have indeed seen most of the cities of this world, but I have found none to compare with Stambul and Galata."

The Shah allowed this to pass, and continued: "At how many Tumens doest thou estimate the combined income of the Beys and Beylerbeys of Turkey?" to which I replied: "The Beys and Beylerbeys of Turkey receive payment according to their rank but they enjoy besides this generally a private income. Other princes remunerate their officers in proportion to the pay of the regiment which they command, but if the pay of the Beys and other officers in the service of the Emperor of Turkey were to be based upon this foundation, it would run not into Tumens nor yet Laks but into Kulurs [2]. To give you an example: The payments made to the Beylerbeys of Rumelia, Anatolia, Egypt, Hungary (Budin = Ofen), Diarbekir, Bagdad, Yemen, and Algiers, are, each in themselves, as much as any other prince would lay out on the whole of his army. This proportion holds good for all the other Beylerbeys also, and is in strict accordance

[1] Lak = £ 100.000, a sum only used in India. [2] See note 3, page 47.

with the superior standing of our government. Quite a different system is adopted for the troops under Khans and Sultans, for there is always an element of uncertainty there; but in Turkey the army belongs to the Padishah. All Beylerbeys and officers are his servants and an Imperial command is law and can not be trifled with[1]."

On this same occasion some of the officers asked whether the documents which had been taken from me by Ibrahim Mirza in Meshhed had ever been placed before the Shah. This question was answered in the affirmative, but I did not like to pursue the subject, mindful of the saying: "When evil slumbers, cursed be he who rouses it" — and I turned the conversation into another channel.

I preferred to plead my cause with another Ghazel which the Shah graciously accepted, and which finally led to the desired result. We received permission to leave. He wrote a letter expressive of his unalterable respect and devotion to his Majesty the Padishah, gave me more presents, and com-

1 Our author refers here to the Feudal system still in use in Central Asia at the time that I was there, and he rightly criticises the limited power of the rulers, which is the necessary result of it. In Persia the relation between the Khans and the Shah was based upon this principle still quite within modern times. The Sultans of Turkey, when in the Zenith of their power, were absolute sovereigns of their land. But at the commencement of the decline the same relationship was established there, as we see from the conduct of the Derebeys.

manded Nazr Bey, a brother of Yūzbashi Hasan Bey, to accompany me on the journey.

While in Kazvin I made a pilgrimage to the grave of Imam Shahzade Husein, and in the beginning of Rebiul Evvel I started on my journey to Bagdad.

Near to Sultani, we passed Abhar, and I stopped to visit the grave of Pir Hasan the son of Akhi Avran, then on to Kirkan (?) where I visited the grave of Mohammed Demtiz [1] a son of Khodja Ahmed Jesewi, and from there to Derghezin and Hamadan in which latter place the graves of Ain-ul-Kuzat and Pir Ebulalay, the armour-bearers of the Prophet, were visited. At Saadabad, our next station, I was met by the governor, who treated me with marked attention.

Then we took our way by Mount Elvend and Nihavend (in Suristan) to Bisutun, where I visited the grave of Kiazim, and in the village Weis-ul-karn, the grave of the Saint of that name. We then proceeded to Kasri-Shirin and through Kurdistan to the fortress Zendjir. While there we were much interested in watching a Humabird [2] high up in the sky. This is

[1] Demtiz = some one possessing strong, i. e. active or powerful dem or nefes = breath.

[2] Huma, name of a mythical bird, a kind of Phoenix, which, as the legend says, lives in the air and never touches the earth, and is held to be a good omen. Thus for inst. anyone who has been overshadowed by this bird is destined to be a ruler. Hence the word "Humayun" = Imperial, an epithet applied to royal persons.

supposed to be a good omen, and we were therefore well pleased. Some enlarged upon the good fortune presaged by his appearance, others spoke of the curious properties of the bird, of whom Saadi sings:

> "The Huma is distinguished from all other birds,
> In that he lives on bones, yet is not a bird of prey."

It is a known fact that this bird feeds exclusively on bones. The legend says that the Huma, before demolishing a bone, carries it up high in the air, and then drops it with the result that it breaks into many pieces. He then swoops down upon these, divides them into equal portions and devours them. This is the origin of the saying, when Persian officials, through extortion, obtain more then they can well digest: "They should follow the example of the Humabird and divide their spoils into smaller, equal portions."

Here, at Zendjir, I dismissed Nazr Bey, whom the Shah had given me as an escort, and after crossing the great river Tokuz Olum [1] (?) we came to Ban(or Sheri Ban). Towards the end of the same month of Rebiul Sani, we reached Bagdad where we were most hospitably received by Khizr Pasha. We did not delay however but hurried on to Turkey.

[1] Tokuz Olum = nine fords (if Olum be taken for the Turkoman word of the same meaning), is not known as the name of a great river, because, besides the Tigris, there are no large rivers in the neighbourhood of Bagdad.

XVII.

The rest of our Adventures.

In the beginning of Djemazi-ul Evvel we crossed the Tigris in ships, and after revisiting the sacred graves there, we journeyed on. Past Kasri, Semke, and Harbi we came to Tekrit and Mossul, and by the old road of Mossul and Djizre to Nisibin. From there by Diarbekir and Mardin we reached Amed, where I saw Iskender Pasha who received me most graciously. In the course of conversation I told him some of our adventures, to which he listened with much interest and exclaimed: "You have gone through more than even Tamum Dari has done, and as for all the marvellous things which you have seen, they are beyond the dreams of even Balkiah and Djihan Shah."

Questioned upon the different sovereigns and armies of the countries I had visited, I said: "In all the world there is no country like Turkey, no sovereign like our Padishah, and no army like the Turkish. From East to West the fame of the Ottoman troops has spread. For victory follows their banner wherever they go. May God keep Turkey in wealth and prosperity until the last day shall dawn. May He preserve our Padishah in health and happiness and our troops ever victorious. Amen!"

When asked whether our name was known in those remote parts, I answered. "Certainly, more than you would think."

In the further course of conversation I learned that a report of my death had reached the Porte, and that therefore the post of Egyptian Admiral had been given to Kurdzade the Sandjak-bey of Rhodus. I thought to myself: "Long live my Padishah, I shall easily obtain another office;" and I comforted myself with poetic effusions. Of course I trusted in God Almighty, nevertheless I was always thinking about the conquest of Ormuz and Gujarat, and I argued thus to myself: "These fantastic dreams have so filled thy brain, that thou art being drawn down to the earth by them; the spirit of wandering is so strong in thee that thou canst not give thy body rest until it shall return to dust."

I resumed my journey to Turkey, in the hope soon to set eyes again on Constantinople. Arrived in Arghini I visited the grave of the prophet Zilkefl; from there by Kharput to Malatia and the grave of Seid Ghazi Sultan, a native of that place, and shortly after I reached Siwas, the first station on Turkish territory. Ali Pasha received me there with marked distinction; I delayed a short time to visit the grave of Abdul Wahab Ghazi, and to call upon Ali Baba, who gave me his blessing.

After this I continued my journey to Stambul, across the plain of Ken to Kara Hissar Behram Shah and through Bozauk to Hadji Bektash, where I made pilgrimages to the graves of the Saint of that place, and of Balam Sultan; then on to Kirshehr and the graves of Hadji Avran and Aashik Pasha, past Ayas Varsak to Angora, crossing the Kizil Irmak (Halys) by the bridge of Chashneghir [1]. I visited the grave of Hadji Bairam Sultan and his children, and the Khidr, and had a friendly interview with Djenabi Pasha. From Beybazari we came to Boli, touched Modurn, and on to Kunik where is the grave of Sheikh Shemseddin; next we came to Tarakli Yenidje and Keive, with the bridge over the Sakaria river, past Agadj-Deniz, on to Sabandja and Iznikmid [2] and the grave of Nebi Khodja. From there our way led past Ghekivize and Skutari, where I crossed the Bosphorus, and reached Constantinople in safety.

God be praised who led me safely through manifold dangers, and brought me back to this most beautiful country of all the earth. Four years have passed away; years of much sorrow and misery, of many privations and perplexities; but now in this year 964 (1556) in the beginning of Redjeb I have

[1] Chashneghir = Cup-bearer, probably the name of the builder.

[2] Iznikmid, now Ismid, has better preserved the ancient Greek name.

once more returned to my own people, my relations, and my friends. Glory and praise be to God the Giver of all good things!

His Majesty the Padishah happened to be at Adrianople, and on the second day after my return I travelled thither, to pay him homage. I had the good fortune to be most graciously received by his Imperial Majesty. The high Viziers and especially Vizier Rustem Pasha, loaded me with kindnesses. I was appointed to join the Corps of the Muteferrika (officers in attendance on the Sultan) with a daily income of sixty aktche. And the Ketkhuda (Intendant), who had accompanied me on my travels, had his salary increased with 8 aktche, and was appointed Muteferrika for Egypt. One of the Bölük-Bashi (Chef d'Escadron) received eight aktche and my other travelling companions each six aktche above their ordinary pay. One of these latter was nominated to the post of Egyptian Tchaush and the others joined the volunteers. They received their pay[1] for the four years they had been away, payment being made out of the Egyptian treasury.

Towards the end of Rajab his Majesty the Sultan

[1] In the text the words علوفه ulufe, عايق ajik, and جرايه have been used. The first means pension and pay, the second is unknown to me and is possibly a misprint, while the third means payment in general.

returned to Constantinople and on the day that he entered the Konak of Tchataldja I was appointed Defterdar of Diarbekir[1]. Thus in his gracious kindness his Majesty had pleased and satisfied us all.

He who wishes to profit by this narrative let him remember that not in vain aspirations after greatness, but in a quiet and contented mind lieth the secret of the true strength which perisheth not. But if in God's providence he should be driven from home, and forced to wander forth in the unknown, and perchance be caught in the turbulent waves of the sea of adversity, let him still always keep in mind that love for one's native land is next to one's faith. Let him never cease to long for the day that he shall see his native shores again, and always, whatever befall, cling loyally to his Padishah.

He who doeth this, shall not perish abroad; God will grant him his desire both in this world and in the next, and he shall rejoice in the esteem and the affection of his fellow-countrymen.

I completed this narrative in Galata in the month Shaaban of the year 964 (1556), and the transcript of it was accomplished in the month Safar of the year 965 (1557).

1 Timar Defterdarlighi = Superintendent of the finances of the army.

INDEX OF PROPER NAMES AND PLACES.

Aashik Pasha, 105.
Aazam, Imam, (Ebn Hanifa), 97.
Abdi-birun, Khodja, 72.
Abdi-derum, Khodja, 72.
Abdul Azim, Imam, 92.
Abdul Kadir Ghilani, Sheikh, 6.
Abdul Khalik, 73.
Abdul Sultan, 77.
Abdullah Khan, 82.
Abdullah, Khodja, 72.
Abdullatif, Sheikh, 69, 79, 96.
Abdul Vahab, Sheikh, 39.
Abdul Vahab Ghazi, 104.
Abdurrahman Bey, 50.
Abdurrahman-bin-Anf, 8.
Abhar, 101.
Abraham, 6.
Abulgazi, 84.
Abul-Maali, Shah, 46.
Abyssinia, 18.
Adam, 6.
Adam Khan, 63.
Aden, 3.
Adil Khan, 30.
Adjul, 7.
Adrianople, 106.
Agadj-Deniz, 105.
Agatai Khan, 80.
Agra, 46, 49.
Ain-ul-Kuzat, 101.
Ahmed, 28.
Ahmed, Sultan, 24, 25, 27, 28, 29, 33.
Ahmed Jesewi, 71, 96, 101.

Ahmed Magrebi, Sheikh, 32.
Ahmed Tchaush, 70, 81.
Ahmedabad, 26, 28, 30, 31, 35.
Ais bin Ishak, 6.
Akhi Avran, 101.
Akil, Imam, 7.
Akserayi, Ibrahim, 3.
Ala-ed-Dowleh Semnani, Sheikh, 91.
Alem, Sadr, 71, 72.
Alemshah Reis, 14.
Aleppo (Haleb), 2, 3, 5, 52.
Algiers, 99.
Ali, Aga, 30.
Ali Baba, 104.
Ali Bey, 89, 93.
Ali Bey, Khan, 73.
Ali bin Husein, Sidi, (Sidi Ali Reïs), 5.
Ali-el-Hadi, Imam, 6.
Ali Hamadani, 67.
Ali, Kamber, 6, 7.
Ali, Khalifa, 6, 7, 8, 33, 71, 86, 88.
Ali Musa Riza, Imam, 78, 86.
Ali Pasha, 104.
Ali, Pir, 93.
Ali Rametin, Sheikh, 79.
Ali Shir, Mir, 50.
Ali Sultan, 84, 85.
Amed, 103.
Anatolia, 99.
Anderab, 66.
Angora, 105.
Arghini, 104.
Argun, 39.
Arslan Mirza, 81.
Ashik, 6.
Ashkabad, 85.
Askeri, Haman, 6.
Astrakhan, 80, 81, 96.
Ata, Hekim, 79.
Ata, Seid, 73.
Attar, Sheikh, 90.
Autchi, see Utchi,
Awhad-ed-din Kirmani, 3.
Ayas Varsak, 105.
Ayesha, 97, 98.
Azerbaidjan, 94.

Baba, Sheikh, 96.
Baber, 66, 67.
Bab-i-Mandeb, 3.
Babu, Mir, 62.
Bachuvara (Bachrewan?), 58.
Badakhshan, 66, 67.
Badjgah, 65.
Bagdad, 1, 6, 7, 82, 94, 99, 101.
Baghi-Feth, 37.
Bagwai, 85.
Bahadur, Sultan, 26, 43.
Baha-eddin Nakishbendi, 78.
Baha-ed-din Zade, 3.
Baha-eddin, Zekeria, 46.
Bahara, 62.
Bahrein, 4, 9, 10.
Bahr-itch, 61.
Bairam Khan, 56, 58.
Bakar, 40, 41.
Bakhtar Zemin (Bakhtar-land or Bactria), 63.
Balam Sultan, 105.
Balkh, 1, 66, 69.
Balkiah, 3, 103.
Balotra, see Belodra.
Ban (or Sheri Ban), 102.
Barkhat, 3.
Baroda, 42.
Bashi, Khodja, 52.
Basrah, 1, 4, 5, 7, 26.
Batum Baku, 96.
Bawerd (Abiwerd), 85.
Bayana, 46.
Bayazid Bestami, 91.
Bazar No, 68.
Bedakhshan, 1.
Behram Mirza, 86, 90.
Behlul Khan, 35.
Behlul Divane, 6.
Belodra (or Balotra), 31.
Beluchistan, 16.
Bender-Lahuri, 38.
Bender Semti (now Semti), 67.
Bengal, 35.
Besai, 27.
Beshr-Hafi, 6.
Bestam, 91.
Beybazari, 105.
Bire, 6.
Biredjik, 5.

Bisutun, 101.
Bokhara, 70, 72, 73, 75, 76, 77, 97.
Boli, 105.
Bombay, 42.
Borak Khan (Noruz Ahmed), 67, 69, 70, 72, 77, 80, 87, 96.
Bosphorus, 105.
Bozauk, 105.
Budin-Ofen (Hungary), 99.
Budjuga Khan, 79.
Bukkur, 42.
Burham-ed-din, Sheikh, 3.
Burham Seid Khan, 69, 70, 72, 73, 74, 75, 76.
Burudj or Broatsh, 26, 27, 31, 33.

Cabul, see Kabul.
Cambay, 22.
Caspian Sea, 82, 84.
Cathiawar or Kathiawar, 19, 20, 37, 42.
Catif or Katif, 4, 9.
Champanir, 31.
Charik, 9.
Charsui, 68.
Chasneghir, 105.
Cherkes, 32.
Circassia, 83.
Constantinople, 2, 5, 48, 52, 96, 104, 105, 107.
Crimea, 53.

Dadash, 69.
Dalli, 67.
Daman, 22, 23, 24, 25, 27.
Damgan, 91.
Daniel, 71.
Daud, 3.
Daud Tagi, Sheikh, 6.
Davud Kaissari, 3.
Delhi, 46, 47, 57.
Demavend-range, 91.
Demir-Kapu, 83.
Dendanshiken, 65.
Derghezin, 101.
Deshti-Kipchak, 1, 79—84.
Diarbekir, 99, 103, 107.
Dible, 42.
Dinar, Malik, 16.
Div (Diu), 20, 22, 27.

Djadi, 10.
Djafar, Imam, 91.
Djamher (Djamkher), 19.
Djar Ullah Ulama, 79.
Djash (Jask), 15.
Djehlam, 63.
Djelaleddin Ekber, see Ekber.
Djelaleddin, Malik, 16.
Djelali, Sheikh, 45.
Djemali, Sheikh, 39, 45.
Djenghelistan, 44.
Djerdjis, 6.
Djihan Shah, 103.
Djihanghir, Ali Khan, 28, 68.
Djilgar, 10.
Djisr (?), 6.
Djizre, 103.
Djoona or Junaghar, 37.
Djugd, 18.
Djumerd-Kassab, 6.
Djuneid Bagdadi, 6.
Djushai, 63.
Dorum (Derum), 85.
Dost Mohammed Khan, 79, 82, 83.
Duabe, 73.
Duldul, 7.
Duspul (Dizful), 9.
Duyuli-Sindi, 38.

Ebn Hifz Kebir, 78.
Ebubekr, Khalipha, 86.
Ebulalay, Pir, 101.
Ebulhasan Harkani, 91.
Ebul Maali, Shah, 56, 59, 62.
Ebu Mansur Matridi, 71.
Egypt, 32, 99.
Ekber, Djelaleddin, 56, 58, 62.
Elvend, Mount, 101.
Enderab, 65.
Esed, Melik, 24, 25.
Esh Sultan, 79, 84, 85.
Euphrates, 5, 7.
Eyub, 78.

Farab, 78.
Faris, Selmas, 7.
Fazil-bin-Ayaz, 6.
Fedzna, 12.
Feizabad, 67.

Ferashi, 65.
Ferid Shekr-Ghendj, Sheikh, 53.
Ferrukh, Mirza, 41.
Ferrukh Fal, Mirza, 64.
Ferrukh Pasha, 96.
Feth Mosuli, 6.
Firdusi, 85.
Firuzshah, 46, 47.
Fischt-Kidsur, 22.
Furmeyan or Formyan, 19, 27.

Galata, 5, 99, 107.
Ghazi Bey, 87.
Ghekivize, 105.
Ghidjduvan, 73.
Goa, 20, 27, 33.
Guador, 16, 17.
Gujarat, 1, 21, 23—35, 48, 52, 104.

Hadjar, 9.
Hadji Avran, 105.
Hadji Bairam Sultan, 105.
Hadji Begum, 40.
Hadji Bektash, 105.
Hadji Mohammed Sultan, 80.
Hadjim Khan, 79.
Haidar, Sultan, 43.
Haladj-Mansur, 6.
Hamadan, 1, 101.
Hambali, Imam, 6.
Hamid, Sheikh, 46.
Hamsa, Aga, 25.
Harbi, 6, 103.
Hasan, 6.
Hasan Basri, 8.
Hasan, Kara, 52.
Hasan Khan, 28.
Hasan, Pir, 101.
Hasan Sultan, Mirmiran Mirza, 46.
Hashim Sultan, 69.
Hasinia, 7.
Herat, 92.
Hezareland (Hezare), 64.
Hezaresp(Hezarus), 78, 84.
Hilla, 7.
Hind, 1, 59.
Hindu Kush, 65.
Hindustan, 45—63.
Hissar-i-Shadman, 68.

Humayun, Padishah, 39, 41, 42, 44, 46, 48, 52, 53, 54.
Humayun, Shah, 38,
Husein, 6.
Husein Dehlevi, Mir, 54.
Husein, Imam, 92.
Husein, Imam Shahzade, 101.
Husein Kharezmi, Molla, 79.
Husein Shah, Mirza, 37, 38, 39, 40, 41, 42.
Husein, Sheikh, 80.
Hussein, Aga, 29.
Huweiza, 8.

Ibn-Batuta, 81.
Ibrahim, Mirza, 66, 86, 87, 100.
Ibrahim Sefevi, Mir, 97.
Ibrahim, Sheikh, 45.
Imare Bugazi, 7.
Imad-ul-Mulk, 32.
Indus (Sihun), 37, 42.
Irak or Irak-Adjem, 82, 83, 90—102.
Iran, 1.
Isa, Khan, 38.
Isa, Mir, 39, 40, 41, 42.
Isa Terkhan, 37.
Iskender (Alexander the Great), 51.
Iskender Khan, 46.
Iskender Pasha, 103.
Ismail Mirza, 92.
Ismail Sultan, 78.
Ivan Wassilyewich, Czar, 80.
Iznikmid (Ismid), 105.

Jedda, 3.
Jodpur (Radjhputana), 31.
Joshua (the Prophet), 6.

Kabul or Cabul, 46, 58, 61, 62, 63, 64, 65.
Kabul (river), 63.
Kabulistan 63—66.
Kaffa, 52, 82.
Kala, 73.
Kalai Zafar, 67.
Kalhat (Calatu), 12.
Kalhata, 9.

Kandahar, 43, 58.
Kara Hissar Behram Shah, 105.
Kara or Kere (Gharra) 45.
Karabag, 65.
Karakul or Karakol, 70, 76, 78.
Karwitch, 46.
Kashgar, 59, 67.
Kasri Semke, 103.
Kasri-Shirin, 101.
Kassarie, 3.
Kavadian, 67.
Kazi Khan, 78.
Kazib-elban-Mosuli, 6.
Kazvin or Kazwin, 1, 83, 92, 101.
Keimzar or Leïme, 10.
Keive, 105.
Kelal, Seid Mir, 78.
Kelnor, 58.
Kemal Aga, 90.
Ken, 105.
Kerbela (Azwie), 6.
Kerman, 15.
Kermineh, 73.
Ketbaye, 27.
Khaiber Pass, 63.
Khaireddin Pasha (Barbarossa), 5, 33.
Khalweti Yan, Sheikh, 79.
Khanate, 73.
Khanka, 84.
Kharcha (Pergenei Kharcha), 48.
Kharezm, 1, 70, 78, 79, 81, 82, 84, 85, 96.
Kharezm Shah, 72, 73, 77.
Kharput, 104.
Khatlan, 1, 66—67.
Khidr, 9.
Khiva (Khiwah), 78, 79, 80, 82, 83.
Khizr Pasha, 102.
Khokand, 50.
Khorasan, 1, 78, 82, 83, 84—90.
Khorfakan (Khorfekan), 12.
Khoshab, 63.
Khoshhal Bey, 50, 57.
Khosru Dehlevi, Mir, 53, 54.
Khosru Shah, 67.

Khotl, 67.
Khudavend, 28, 30.
Khyber Pass, see Khaiber Pass.
Kiazim, Imam Muza, 6, 101.
Kibla, 52.
Kichi Mekran, 15.
Kihmerd Bey, 62.
Kirkan (?), 101.
Kirnat (Karnal), 57.
Kirghiz-steppe, 80.
Kirshehr, 105.
Kis, 10.
Kishm, 67.
Kizilbash, 83.
Kizil Irmak (Halys), 105.
Kökche Khalipha, 86, 93, 95.
Konia, 2.
Kubad Pasha, 4.
Kuduri, Sahib, 79.
Kufa, 6.
Kulaba (Kulab), 67.
Kunduz, 67.
Kunik, 105.
Kurdistan, 101.
Kurdzade, 104.
Kutbeddin Shah, 53.
Kuvva or Kuva, 12.

Laghman (Lughman), 64.
Lahore, 43, 46, 53, 57, 58, 59, 61.
Lahsa, 9.
Ludiana, 58.

Maaruf Kerkhi, 6.
Maashuk, 6.
Maasum Bey, 93, 94.
Machvara, 45.
Mahmud Khan, 35.
Mahmud, Sultan, 38, 40, 41, 42, 43, 49, 80, 85.
Mahmudabad, 32.
Makhdum Aazam, 80.
Malatia, 104.
Mangit or Manghit (tribe), 72, 80.
Mankut (or Mankit), 46, 58.
Mardin, 103.
Masib, 6.
Maskat or Muscat, 3, 12.

Matchi, 42.
Matchuvara (Matchivara), 58.
Mav, 44.
Mazar, 69.
Maz-enderan, see Mazendran.
Mazendran, 91.
Mecca, 22, 52, 96.
Medain, 7.
Medina, 52.
Mehemmed Hekim Mirza, 64.
Mehemmed, Molla Pir, (Mohammed, Pir), 58.
Mehzari, 9.
Mekran, 25.
Memi, Hadji, 29.
Memi, Kalfat, 14.
Menglir (Manglaus or Menglaur?), 19.
Mervan, 65.
Merw, 85.
Meshhed, Khodja, 78.
Meshhed, 1, 82, 85, 86, 93, 100.
Minar, 74.
Minglur, 27.
Miri, Sheikh, 39.
Mirza the Wise, Khan, 66.
Mirza Shah, 46, 58.
Misra, 7.
Modurn, 105.
Mohammed Aftah, 91.
Mohammed Bari'i, Imam, 79.
Mohammed Bey, 93.
Mohammed Demtiz, 101.
Mohammed Garabili, Sheikh, 6.
Mohammed Ghazali, Imam, 6.
Mohammed Hanifi, Imam, 9, 85.
Mohammed, Imam, 6, 9.
Mohammed Khan, Pir, 66, 69, 70.
Mohammed Khudabend, 92.
Mohammed Mahruk, Imam-zade, 90.
Mohammed Mehdi, Imam, 7.

Mohammed Radjva, Sheikh, 46.
Mohammed Taki, Imam, 6.
Molla-Bi, 57.
Molla-i-Rumi, 2.
Mossul, 6, 103.
Muhieddin, Sheikh, 8.
Multan, 45.
Mun'im Khan, 64, 65.
Munshi, Mir, 93, 95.
Murad Bey, 4.
Muradabad, 46.
Musa Khan, 35.
Mustafa, Aga, 30.
Mustafa Bey, Derzi, 14.
Mustafa, Kara, 14.
Mustafa Pasha, 7, 8, 10.
Mutawali, 86, 87, 88, 89.

Nasirpur (Nasirabad), 40.
Nasir-ul-Mulk, 26, 27, 28.
Nasrabad, 38.
Nasreddin, Khodja, 86.
Naushar, 42.
Nazr Bey, 101, 102.
Nebi, Khodja, 105.
Nedjd, 14.
Nedjef (Haira), 6.
Nedjmeddin Kubera, 79.
Nerbudda, 26.
Nesa, 85.
Nezri, Mir, 65, 66.
Nihavend, 101.
Nilab, 63.
Nisebin, 6, 103.
Nishabur, 90.
Nishapur see Nishabur.
Nizam, Sheikh, 35.
Nizam Weli, Sheikh, 53.
Noah, 6.
No Bazar, see Bazar No.
Obeidullah, 69.
Ofen, 52.
Oman, 3, 12.
Omar, Khalipha, 86.
Ormuz, 3, 4, 7, 8, 9, 10, 11, 15, 32, 104.
Osman, Khalipha, 86.
Oxus, 67, 78, 84.

Pani-Pata (Panipat), 57.
Parker (Parkar or Nagar-Parkar), 36.
Patna, 35.

Patri, 42.
Pehlevan Mahmud Pir, 78.
Pendje, 67.
Pendjkend, 45.
Pendj-Mahal, 31.
Penjab, 47, 58.
Pershuer (Peshawer), 63.
Persia, 83.
Pervane, 65.
Peshai, 65.
Piri Bey, 3.
Piri Pasha, 56.
Pulad Sultan, 85.
Pul-i-Senghin, 68.
Pul Rabat, 73.

Radanpoor (Radhanpur), 35.
Ras Dibba, 12.
Rauzat es Sefa, 83.
Rei, 92, 93.
Reis, Murad, 10.
Reïs, Sidi Ali, 84, 85, 88, 91.
Reis, Suleiman, 4.
Reis, Rejeb, 4.
Reka (Orfah), 5.
Rhodes, 5.
Rishehr (Bushir?), 9.
Rukneddin, 46.
Rum, 51.
Rumelia, 99.
Rustak, 67.
Rustem Pasha, 106.

Saad, 3.
Saadabad, 101.
Saadi, 102.
Sabandja, 105.
Sadi-es Sueiba, 7.
Sadkere, 46.
Sadr Alem, 80.
Sadreddin, 46.
Sadr-ed-din-Koniavi, Sheikh, 2.
Sadr-esh-Sheriat, 78.
Sahib Kuduri, 79.
Sahrand, 46.
Sahrandi, 58.
Sahranpur, 19.
Said, 3.
Sakaria (river), 105.
Sakkars, 58.
Salih, Mir, 39, 41.

Samani, 57.
Samarkand, 69, 70, 71, 81, 82.
Sambal, see Senbel.
Samira, 6.
Samiri, 24.
Sani-Pata (Sonpat), 57.
Saraidjik, 81.
Sarakhsi, 78.
Sebzeghiran, 93.
Sebzevar, 90.
Sehri-Sebz (Kesh), 69.
Seid Ghazi, Sultan, 104.
Selim Shah 46, 58.
Selim, Sultan, 56.
Semke, 6.
Semtche, 42.
Senbel (Sambal) 46.
Senghirdek (Seng-ghirdek), 68.
Seri' Sakati, 6.
Sevindek, Aga, 92.
Sewalik, 58.
Shafi, Imam, 97.
Shahab-ed-din Sohraverdi, Sheikh, 6.
Shahar, 3.
Shahin Bey, 54, 55.
Shah-Zinde, 71.
Sham, 81.
Shar, 17.
Sheba (Shabar), 15.
Shefata, 6.
Shehri Sebz, 70.
Sheibani Khan, 67.
Shemseddin, Sheikh, 105.
Shemsi-Tebrizi, 2.
Sherifi Pasha, 9.
Shibli, Sheikh, 6.
Shimun, 6.
Shiraz, 9.
Shir Khan, 35, 46.
Shirvan, 82,
Shiyul, 27.
Shushter, 9.
Sidi-Ghazi, 2.
Sihun, see Indus,
Sinan Pasha, 5.
Sind, 1, 18, 36—45, 59.
Siyawan (Sehivan?), 42.
Siwas, 51.
Skutari, 105.
Sohar, 12.

Sonpat, see Sani-Pata,
Stambul, 99.
Suez, 3.
Sufism, 79.
Suleiman, Mirza, 86.
Suleiman, Shah, 66.
Suleiman, Sultan, 1, 5, 83.
Sultani, 101.
Sultanpoor, 44, 47.
Sumenat (Somenat or Somnath), 19, 27.
Surat, 25, 26, 27, 28, 36.
Sutlej, 45.

Tadj esh Sheriat, 78.
Tak Kesri, 7.
Talha, 8.
Talikan, 66.
Tamum Dari, 103.
Tani Sera (Tanesar), 57.
Tarakli Yenidje, 105.
Tarkhan, 40.
Tashkend, 70.
Tata (Tatta or Thats), 37, 39, 40, 41.
Tchaganian (Hissar-i-Shadman), 68.
Tchar Bekir, 78.
Tchardjui (Tchihar-djui), 74, 84.
Tcharikar, 65.
Tchataldja, 107.
Tchiharshembe, 68.
Tebriz, 94, 96.
Teheran, 92.
Tëir, 6.
Tekrit, 6, 103.
Termed, 67.
Thamasp Shah, 83.
Theodosia (see Kaffa),
Tigris, 6, 102, 103.
Timur Sultan, 68, 71, 72, 80.
Tin Sultan, 84, 85,
Tokuz Olum (?), 102.
Transoxania, 1, 67, 68.
Trimba, 45.
Tugbeghi, 39.
Turan, 1, 68—78.
Turkestan, 70.
Tus, 85.

Urghendj, 81.
ul-Ulema, Sultan, 2.

Umad-el?Mulk, 25.
Uns-bin-Malik, 8.
Ural, 81.
Utchi or Autchi (Utsch), 45.

Van, 94.
Vasit, 7.
Vezir, 79, 85.
Vienna, 52.
Volga, 81, 96.

Wafkend, 73.
Wanga (Wanna?), 37.
Weis-ul-Karn, 101.

Yaakub Tcharkhi, 68.
Yagmur, 29.
Yari, Molla, 39, 42, 49.
Yemen, 3, 52, 99.
Yunis, 6.
Yussuf, Imam, 6.
Yüzbashi Hasan Bey, 96, 101.

Zabulistan, 1.
Zakeriah, 3.
Zekya, 7.
Zenan, Shah, 7.
Zendjir, 101, 102.
Zerefshan (or Kohik), 73.
Zilkefl, 7.
Zobëir, 8.
Zofar or Dhofar, 17.